MW01030634

# MEDICAL WARRIOR

## FIGHTING CORPORATE
## SOCIALIZED MEDICINE

## MIGUEL A. FARIA, JR., M.D.

Hacienda Publishing
Macon, Georgia

Grateful acknowledgment is made to the *Journal of the Medical Association of Georgia* and Susan T. Johnson, Interim Editor (now Managing Editor of the *Journal*) and the *Medical Sentinel* of the Association of American Physicians and Surgeons for permission to reprint previously published material.

Hacienda Publishing
Macon, Georgia
Copyright ©1997 by Miguel A. Faria, Jr., M.D.

First Edition.
All Rights Reserved.

1 3 5 7 9 10 8 6 4 2

Library of Congress Catalog Card Number: 97-072144
ISBN: 0-9641077-2-4

Printed and bound in the United States of America on acid-free paper.

# CONTENTS

# PREFACE

From the outset, I want to take the opportunity to introduce the reader to a resurgent, vigorous, and inspiring organization:
the Association of American Physicians and Surgeons (AAPS). This is
the national medical organization to which I had the honor of
speaking at their 51st Annual Meeting (1994) in anticipation of the
publication of my first book, *Vandals at the Gates of Medicine—
Historic Perspectives on the Battle over Health Care Reform.*
Whether you are a physician or not, you need to be acquainted with
this organization. As you will remember, during the heat of the great
health care debate (1992-1994) and before the dust had settled, it
was the AAPS that brought to light the behind-the-scenes activities
of President Bill Clinton's Health Care Task Force, and through a
widely publicized lawsuit, revealed the task force was operating in
violation of the Sunshine Laws (the Federal Advisory Committee Act
[FACA]) and in utter disregard of the rule of law.

Let me also remind you, almost without exception, at the
state level and particularly at the national level, it has been the AAPS
that has stood firm, time and again—representing, uncompromis-
ingly, the rank and file physicians in the trenches and the needs of
their patients, the sanctity of the patient-doctor relationship, and the
practice of private medicine. I'm also happy to state for the record
that for this purpose, in the Spring of 1996, the AAPS launched a new
publication in medical journalism: the *Medical Sentinel*—it's official
journal, to tackle socioeconomic and political issues affecting medicine, even if they are deemed politically incorrect or controversial
by the entrenched medical political establishment.

The AAPS, with its courageous publications, informative
fax, and the venue of the courts, has stood up repeatedly to fight for
the individual rights of practicing physicians and their patients,
while other national organizations vacillated, capitulated; or in their
economic interest, found it easier to ride the waves of anticipated
change while their purported leaders attempted unsuccessfully to
take a vacuous seat at (but ended only taking the scraps thrown at
them from) the table.

Yes, many other national organizations found it easier
during the momentous health care debate of 1993, to go with the

flow, erroneously convinced that socialized medicine was an irresistible, ineluctable force that could not be stopped. So convinced, dozens of medical organizations in pragmatic fashion (and mind you, for the most part, without polling their members) jumped onto, and rode securely, in the bandwagon of political expediency and political correctness, aiding and abetting the changes being brought about, step-by-step, by government-dictated medicine. Although, the American Medical Association (AMA) to its only credit did not endorse the Health Security Act of 1993, it played no part in its demise—not like the grassroots, small businesses, independent insurers and other political organizations—not to mention the AAPS, and the American people, finally acting as informed and vigilant citizenry.

From the beginning, the AAPS rejected the Clinton plan, not on the basis of economics, but rather on moral principles. In the battle for health system reform, the AAPS, as a medical organization, almost alone, stood for Hippocratic medicine's idealism and true altruism, dispelling the extortions and distortions of the waves of false government compassion and pseudo-philanthropy. Today, it is again the AAPS that, virtually single-handedly, is fighting managed care/managed competition—the almost uniquely American paradigm of *corporate socialized medicine*.

So, the battle is far from over. Detrimental health care changes, embodied in the notions of managed care/managed competition, are taking place, even as we speak, leading us down the path of *Corporatism.* And don't allow the endless debates on the budget and alleged major Medicare and Medicaid cuts presently raging on Capitol Hill obfuscate your perception and distract you from the real, looming threat and the tragic events taking place in American medicine today. These current events are as much of a threat to the preservation of the sanctity of the patient-doctor relationship, Hippocratic medicine, and patient and physician autonomy, as socialized medicine, in the form of the single-payer system, was two or three years ago. In fact, the failures and short comings of the managed care/managed competition scheme may lead in the end directly to the single-payer system, when the "free-market" is erroneously blamed for the failure and collapse of corporatism in American medicine.

Giant health care networks, insurers and megacorpora-tions—e.g., Aetna, Cigna, Prudential, Metra-Health (and now Blue Cross/Blue Shield)—as well as powerful foundations—(e.g., Henry Kaiser Permanente and the Robert Wood Johnson Foundations) are organizing and consolidating and using their enormous resources so as to eradicate completely the independent practice of private med-icine, the genuinely patient-oriented free-market medical care, while pushing relentlessly for managed competition, Preferred Provider Organizations (PPOs), Health Maintenance Organizations (HMOs), and other profitable forms of managed care, as to create the almost uniquely American paradigm of *corporate socialized medicine*. This is the same strategy that was used so successfully to empower the for-profit bureaucrats of the health networks, acting in collusion with their counterparts in the government and the public sector, to saddle a state like Minnesota, where managed care now reigns supreme, with its own Clinton-style form of corporate socialized medicine.

The point is that practicing physicians, busy as they are, can no longer afford to stay on the sidelines. Together with their informed and now mobilized patients, they must become involved, for they have a civic, professional, and moral obligation to not only become informed and vigilant but do their duty, to preserve the sanctity of the patient-doctor relationship and protect the health care and welfare of their patients, while rejecting the subjugation of the noble and ancient profession of medicine with the shackles of corporatism. And so, we must all ponder the words of John Philpot Curran (1790), "The condition upon which God hath given liberty to man is eternal vigilance; which condition if he breaks, servitude is at once the consequence of his crime and the punishment of his guilt."

Miguel A. Faria, Jr., M.D.

*Macon, Georgia*
*January, 1997*

# PART ONE: LESSONS FROM HISTORY

CHAPTER 1

# A CALL TO ARMS

Corporate socialized medicine euphemistically (and deceptively) denoted managed competition is becoming an unpleasant reality, step-by-step, under the rubric of managed care and the falsely called "free-market." In this light, both Michael Kingsley in *Time* magazine on the Left side of the fence and M. Stanton Evans in *Human Events* from the Right, are sadly but insightfully correct, when they observe and note the similarities between the proposed (and I may add, actually occurring) changes in medical care and the providentially ill-fated, Health Security Act of 1993 of President Bill Clinton.

## A DECEPTIVE ILLUSION

For instance, we have regional alliances (incarnated in the burgeoning managed care megacorporations that place a wedge in the patient-physician relationship), price controls (government-imposed spending limits for Medicare and Medicaid), loss of choice (i.e., these same patients are being herded into managed care plans), and at the very core of these health care changes, we find the same duplicitous centerpiece as the Clinton plan: managed care/managed competition in all its glory and manifestations—including rationing of medical care (i.e., employers selling the medical care of their employees to the lowest bidder), gatekeepers with perverse incentives (e.g., financial rewards for those who ration medical care); those physicians who jump big time into managed care as part owners or administrators are rewarded with huge profits. Unceremoniously, inconspicuously, and conveniently Hippocratic medicine is being thrown out with the bath water for the higher purpose of achieving the bottom line at the expense of uninformed patients.

Despite all the purported (and belated) support for tax-free Medical Savings Accounts (MSAs) by the policy-makers and organized medicine, the fact remains MSAs coupled with high-deductible catastrophic insurance coverage, occupy a secondary position in the health care scheme of things, despite the reality it is the only proposal on the table that relies on individual responsibility and enlightened (consumer-oriented) self-interest.

Thus, still headed in the wrong, managed competition direction; towards a veritable medical gulag of medical care deterioration; loss of patient choice (i.e., choice of physician, place of treatment and health care plan); medical care rationing; loss of patient confidentiality (via coercive medical records disclosure and indiscriminate data collection by third-party payers and the government, the Oath of Hippocrates notwithstanding); and euthanasia,* the ultimate form of rationing—physicians and their patients still face an ominous threat from the changes taking place in American medicine. Suffice to say, the ability of doctors to practice Hippocratic medicine and do all they can for their patients in today's managed care environment is being increasingly challenged.

It is thanks to the *AAPS v. Clinton* (the litigation that challenged the secret dealings of the Health Care Task Force and to which I referred earlier), we have learned that major foundations such as the Henry Kaiser Permanente and Robert Wood Johnson Foundations, and the "Big Five" insurers with their burgeoning networks were acting under monopolistic government protection (and with already pre-existing favorable federal and state tax laws) to promote and impose managed competition/managed care and change the time-honored ethics of the medical profession. Where once the supreme medical ethic dictated that physicians place their individual patients' interest above their own (and above that of the state) in the spirit of true altruism and charity, today's ethics of corporate socialized medicine and managed competition propound and in many instances force physicians to place cost considerations (i.e., under pain of losing their incentive end-of-year bonuses and even their employment) and the interest of third-party payers and the government above that of their patients.

Simply stated: The big health care megacorporations want

---

* Just recently in *Compassion in Dying v. State of Washington*, the 9th Court of Appeals ruled competent, adult terminally ill patients have a constitutional right to physician-assisted suicide, striking down a Washington statute banning such a practice. *AMNews*; 39(12) March 25, 1996. The same court awaits hearings of an Oregon measure passed in November 1994 (by a 51% to 49% margin) legalizing physician-assisted suicide.

physicians to practice what the Swiss philosopher, Professor Ernest Truffer, calls a *veterinary ethic* which rejects the traditional medical ethic requiring a physician to care for his/her patient according to the individual patient's specific medical needs and requirements, in favor of a new ethic which consists of caring for the patient as if he were a sick animal, a mere pet, not in accordance with its specific medical need, but according to the convenience of its master or owner—the person or entity paying the medical bills.

For the first time in the history of medicine, American physicians are being coaxed or coerced, whatever the individual case might be, to subvert their long-held medical ethics to ration health care by restricting their patient's access to specialists or to high-tech, life-saving (and presumably expensive) medical treatments—that is, forced, uninformed, deceptively-contrived, involuntary rationing for the sake of cost containment, and as to make the HMOs, PPOs, or the PHOs (Physicians Hospital Organizations) for which they work, more efficient and profitable.

Physicians today are subject to *economic credentialing*— the methodology and so-called cost-effective analysis by which hospitals and health care networks (particularly HMOs) use utilization review data about physician medical practices (not primarily to determine quality of care as claimed, but more accurately, to monitor physicians' financial impact on their networks). Physicians who have not been cost-effective, that is, they have not been stringent enough in their restrictions (e.g., have not curtailed enough of their patients' utilization of medical care or who treat the sickest and most difficult cases and thereby incur the most costs in their communities), not only may have their bonuses withheld at the end of the year, but could even lose their membership status in hospitals or health care networks when they apply for new, additional, or for renewal of clinical staff privileges. It goes without saying the withholding of bonuses and the threat of losing employment (or lucrative contracts) becomes a powerful incentive for rationing and the withholding of needed medical care.

This dilemma may seem bad enough for doctors, but it's even worse for unwary patients. Ordinary citizens need to know and understand that when their physicians get *delisted* by these networks, they lose their freedom to choose their doctor; when their local hospital is not contracted by these networks, they lose their freedom to choose their place of treatment; and when the bureaucrats decree a treatment or procedure is not "deemed appropriate or medically necessary (that is not cost-effective)," they lose their choice of health or treatment plan. This is not only immoral and unethical medical practice, but it has led to unfair competition played out on an uneven playing field in a mislabeled "free-market."

## A WAY OUT...

The only way out of this quagmire is to go back to Hippocratic medicine; back to putting patients first, and by the implementation of *tax-free medical savings accounts* (MSAs) in health care. And for this to take place, the laws must be changed at the federal and state levels to provide tax equity and truly empower individuals, as responsible citizens and consumers of healthcare. It will also bring down spiraling health care costs voluntarily, via a true, individually-based, competitive marketplace, without compromising a physician's ethics, the patient-doctor relationship, or the patients' right to choose and spend his own health care dollar as he sees fit.

### INFORMED AND VIGILANT CITIZENS

If physicians and their informed patients do not become vigilant and proactive during this precarious and likely transitory period, what we are all going to get as ultimate consumers of health care will be the same reforms as proposed by President Clinton in 1993, only this time they have been repackaged and fallaciously endorsed by moderate legislators and misguided conservatives who should know better, i.e., the difference between an individually-based free-market and the convoluted concept of corporate socialism—corporatism). Thus, we will end up with more of the same, more managed care to satiety, managed care *ad nauseam* and with it, covert rationing of medical care, quality sacrificed under the guise of cost controls, and as I intimated earlier, in the not-too-distant future, government-sanctioned euthanasia for the elderly, not as true benevolent, magnanimous acts of self-determination as proclaimed by leading ethicists (many of them, neither physicians or philosophers, for that matter), but surreptitiously, as we shall see, encouraged by the state as the ultimate form of rationing.

As you probably already know, Oregon has been the first state to attempt to follow the lead of the Netherlands, and as previously mentioned, in November of 1994, passed a referendum permitting physician-assisted suicide, which remains tied up in courts and appeals. Given what we now know about this practice in the Netherlands, extensive judicial review of this measure is wise and appropriate. As the reader may already be aware of, in Holland, active euthanasia or so-called medical "mercy killing," although technically illegal, is already commonplace, practiced by 81% of Dutch family physicians—10 to 15,000 patients are being put to death yearly, some for psychiatric illnesses, many without their explicit consent. Cost controls, rationing, deterioration in the quality of care, and ultimately, euthanasia (whether practiced under eugenics as effected in Nazi Germany, or categorized as self-determination as touted here and in the Netherlands) are all logical steps and intricate facets of socialized medicine. Moreover, rationing in the corporate state means not only "proper allocation of resources" by the state central planners, but huge profits for the networks, working in "partnership" with the government.

(October, 1996)

## CHAPTER 2

# *VANDALS AT THE GATES*

But what events have led us to this deplorable state of affairs with American medicine headed inexorably in the wrong direction—down the path of welfarism, collectivism, and corporatism? To answer this loaded and troublesome question, perhaps one should ponder the words of the politician par excellence, Franklin Delano Roosevelt, who once admitted, "Nothing just happens in politics. If something happens, you can be sure it was planned that way." So, in our search for answers, let us glean and ponder deeply at the changes ushered in the 1960s by the Great Society of President Lyndon B. Johnson.

### A MODERN TROJAN HORSE?

During that time, many people thought government could solve all of their and society's problems. Physicians were no exception. So yes, many physicians succumbed to the allurement of Medicare and Medicaid in 1965. "After all," they asked themselves, "why not accept government payments for medical services formerly provided the indigent as charity, *pro bono publico*?" With these question finally answered in the affirmative by a pragmatic leadership, the physicians listened to the seductive songs of the sirens that weakened their natural defenses to government intrusion. So began the government onslaught that ultimately resulted in the breaching of the walls of the House of Medicine.

Perhaps physicians should have listened to their literary confrere, Dr. Anton Chekhov, who as a devoted Russian physician often worked without payment and once revealed, "I am poor and broke because I thought it desirable for myself and my independence to refuse the remuneration the cholera doctors receive." Suffice it to say, the cholera doctors he referred to were employed by the government. Likewise, today, many physicians are again listening to the alluring sirens of managed care, scurrying about to sign up with this or that network—thinking [that]…"managed care is here to stay, and in any event, if I don't, others will."

Dr. Thomas A. Dorman, a California AAPS member wrote in 1992 in his office practice newsletter, "It seems that we in America are about to embark on an accelerated venture of harnessing the capitalist engine for the destruction of healing...an unholy marriage of corporate capitalism to government bureaucracy." Only this "partnership with government," everyone from President Clinton to Secretary of Labor, Robert Reich are vaunting, is more correctly denoted *corporate socialism*—the same economic arrangement we witnessed in Italy, Germany, and Japan in the pre-World War II era—the economic component of Fascism. Individually-based, patient-oriented, Hippocratic medicine and virtue-based ethics are quietly being pushed aside.

### THE BEGINNING OF THE GREAT AMERICAN DECLINE

Let us now return to the legacy of the Great Society. The government onslaught against American medicine was launched in tandem with the concerted, all-out assault upon the various institutions of American society that (with one notable exception we will mention later) had served America, the land of opportunity, so well.[1] Yes, along with the government inroads made into the edifice of the medical profession, the 1960s also witnessed major changes in the criminal justice system, so that the rights of criminals came to supersede those of the victims. Crime began to pay for itself, and it paid handsomely. And while criminals were pandered by a permissive society which relinquished individual responsibility and moral accountability, gun control became a panacea for growing violence and street crime. The Gun Control Act of 1968, fashioned after Hitler's gun laws of 1938,[2] was passed to compensate for the changing societal mores and the increasingly weakened criminal justice system.

It was also about this time the ethics of the civil justice system (tort) underwent a serious transmogrification. After centuries of a common law tradition, whereby lawsuits were filed only as a measure of last resort, now lawsuits were felt to be good for society, not only as a method of resolving legal disputes, but also as a powerful weapon to effect a more "equitable" wealth redistribution in society.

Malpractice lawsuits became commonplace and reached destructive epidemic proportions. Of course, this redistribution did not affect the large profits made by the attorney-litigators or what the legal scholar Walter Olson has penned, the "sue-for-profit litigation industry."[3] These swashbuckler litigators saw themselves as crusaders stamping out injustice and correcting the alleged perceived evils of American capitalist society. Moreover, in this egalitarian, adversarial, litigious atmosphere, societal contracts were deemed no longer sacred and could be violated with impunity by activist jurists.

The inception of the welfare state of the Great Society heralded the beginning of the great American cultural decline. It was also the beginning of the end of the Golden Age of Medicine and the beginning of the erosion of the independence of American physicians and the previously sacrosanct patient-doctor relationship. And with these lamentable developments, in due time, patients would lose physicians as their true advocates, and with it, the right to expect the best care that their private physicians could provide.

On the economic front, the sweeping reforms ushered in the final devaluations of the currency so that after a series of monetary reforms, beginning in the 1930s with the policies of the Federal Reserve System, U.S. paper money by 1968 (for U.S. citizens) and by 1971 (for foreigners), was no longer backed by (and thus, irredeemable with) gold or silver.[4] The predictable, unrestrained printing of paper money or *fiat currency* by the Federal Reserve, without precious metal backing allowed inflation to become a permanent fixture of the American economy.

Meanwhile, Keynesian economics was accepted by President Richard Nixon and the establishment as an explicit substitute for truly free-market capitalism. The implementation of wage and price controls in 1971 was then used to justify the fight against the inflation the government had created in the first place.

For physicians, their share of the health care budget pie, which has remained unchanged at 19%, meant that with inflation, their real earnings, like everybody else's, were eroding. So, it is not surprising that Medicare and Medicaid, for some, promised a path to financial prosperity. Physicians made more money than ever before with government intervention, but it was at a heavy price, for it carried the hidden cost of their independence.

The reader, no doubt, will be surprised to learn that it was also about this time, in the years 1971 to 1974, that the mechanics of managed competition were worked out with the diligent cooperation of the private and public sectors, and thereby, the sponsorship of both Republican President Richard Nixon and Democratic Senator from Massachusetts, Edward Kennedy. The consensual road was paved as to proceed with the delivery of medical care via Health Maintenance Organizations (HMOs), through the prepaid consumption of medical care via government-approved group practices.* Sen. Kennedy would lead the charge for government intervention in health care through the 1970s and 1980s, and would support the corporate concept of managed competition, hand in hand with, and through the ill-fated attempt at the government takeover of the American health care industry by President Clinton's Health Security Act of 1993, to the end of the century.

Progressive government intervention in every aspect of American society heralded the beginning of the decline of the truly individual-based, free enterprise system, and the erosion of America's sense of self-reliance and rugged individualism. And in my estimation, it also marked the beginning of the ebb of Western civilization and the American way of life.

### THE LEGACY OF THE GREAT SOCIETY

Despite spending $4.5 trillion dollars, on the social front, the War on Poverty, by all estimations, has been an utter failure. In fact, it has worsened the lot of those it had intended to benefit. The traditional family is rapidly disintegrating as families are headed not by fathers, but by the faceless bureaucrats of the nanny state. Illiteracy is rampant, despite public schools and record per-pupil expenditures. Teenage pregnancy and illegitimacy have doubled, tripled, and are still climbing. White illegitimacy is approaching 20% and Blacks 60% (in some inner-cities, it exceeds 80%). Not surprisingly, among the many societal ills, we have been afflicted with a veritable epidemic of premature, low-birth weight infants (along with relatively high U.S. perinatal morbidity and mortality

* A simple concept of HMOs for pre-payment of medical care had been pioneered by industrialist, Henry J. Kaiser, and physician, Sidney Garfield, M.D., in California in the 1930s.

statistics), and consequently, soaring health care costs necessary to care for these infants.

This unfortunate occurrence has been cited as another pretext for government intrusion, but the truth is that this sad state of affairs has nothing to do with the quality of care provided by American physicians, but much to do with societal decay and the loss of individual responsibility.

Likewise, the legacy of the 1960s created a "generation gap" that alienated children from their parents; students from teachers; and not surprisingly, respect for elders and civility were lost. Absolute and universal truths gave way to moral relativism and situational ethics. Immediate gratification and "follow your bliss" philosophy was substituted for hard work, honest living, and deferred gratification. Rugged individualism gave way to the cult of victimhood. A wall of separation was erected between church and state,* and organized prayer was prohibited in public schools.

Earlier, I mentioned a notable exception to the disastrous policies of the 1960s, and indeed, a singular but empyrean zenith was reached with the end of legal discrimination and the eradication of institutionalized racism. But, alas, even the achievements of the civil rights movement (e.g., the Civil Rights Act of 1965) have been turned upside down with the concept of affirmative action and racial quotas which stigmatizes the members of minority groups who have triumphed from the establishment of true equality of opportunity, and has relegated the intended beneficiaries to a perpetual cycle of dependency from which there has been no escape.

The truth is that, no matter what their intentions might have been, the elitist mindset of government bureaucrats has inculcated upon its intended beneficiaries the erroneous idea that they can not succeed without government handouts and the paternalism of the welfare state. This policy, or rather philosophy, sent countless victims down the path of government dependency and onto the demoralizing travails of the liberal plantation, from which (it is worth repeating) there has been no escape.

*The term is derived from a letter written by Thomas Jefferson to the Baptist officials in Danbury, Connecticut (January 1, 1802) in which he did not claim a separation of religion be made from public life, but instead opined his view that the establishment of a state religion was not within the purview of the federal government.[5]

On the political front, it was the beginning of the politics of envy to justify the taking of the fruits of the labors of hard-working individuals (via taxation or otherwise) to give to others, not so predisposed. It was and continues to be redistribution of wealth via institutionalized, legal plunder, on a grand scale. In the meantime, success especially when accompanied by wealth creation (for some who are not as equal as others) became immoral. Yet, all this time, the government was (and continues to be) getting bigger and more intrusive at the expense of productive citizens. With this legacy, it is no wonder that the government bureaucrats are not only consolidating and perpetuating their positions of power and control, but also are dividing and conquering, in Machiavellian fashion, while "inhaling" and imbibing heavily on the divisive and destructive politics of envy.

### MARCHING TO THE DRUMBEAT OF MEDICAL SOCIALISM

On the medical front, we have established how with the inception of Medicare and Medicaid, the government had made its first major incursion into American medicine, and now a precedent had been effectively set for the step-by-step encroachment into the realm of American medicine, the best in the world. In time, a long train of abuses and usurpations followed, and soon swarms of officers, government officials, and sundry vandals began their relentless conquest of the best health care system in the world. Such abuses and usurpations in the late 1980s led to the establishment of what I refer to in a brief but apropos editorial as the *medical gulag*:[6] ineffective price-controls for hospitals via DRGs and for physicians via RBRVS (a methodology derived from the Marxist labor theory of values); behavioral conditioning via Volume Performance Standards (VPS); Big Brother intimidation tactics via perennial threats of Medicare and Medicaid sanctions, and sundry other abuses obstructing the administration of justice in medical practice.

Physicians, especially who refuse to march in lockstep with government edicts, are harassed and intimidated with attestation statements appended to the potential, arbitrary charge of waste, fraud and abuse, and other threats. Violation of these edicts could trigger harsh penalties, civil and criminal asset forfeiture proceedings, and land such "disruptive" physicians in jail.

No documentation was ever provided to support the Inspector General's assertion that fraud and abuse amounted to 10% of health care costs, but we do know that less than 2% of physicians were ever found to be violating Medicare rules and sanctioned. And of those, all have been enticed by government programs and government money. Moreover, utilization review was found to be notoriously cost-ineffective and counterproductive: For every dollar saved, ten dollars were wasted in reviews and administrative costs.[7]

In time, physicians would also have foisted upon them *ex post facto* laws in the case of the Clinical Laboratory Improvement Act (CLIA) and authoritarian and extortionary tactics in the form of Occupational Safety Hazard Administration (OSHA); and all of this, mind you, under the looming threat of the odious and potentially calamitous accusation of waste, fraud and abuse, and civil and criminal asset forfeiture proceedings. To add insult to injury, a charge of this nature would, under the aegis of administrative law, be administered by impersonal bureaucrats who are not restrained by the shackles of constitutional protection.

Consider the predicament: Physicians in the trenches of health care delivery, virtually under siege, bound to obey cryptic laws, deliberately vague and arbitrary, so that Big Brother can call them guilty whenever he likes. And frankly, with HMOs and managed care, ideas conceived at least 30 years ago by government bureaucrats in collusion with willing private entities with a vested financial interest in managed competition, I see no cause for comfort. Practicing physician and their patients should, nevertheless, take solace in Goethe's words,"whosoever, aspiring, struggles on, for him there is salvation."

## HISTORIC PARALLELS: PANEM ET CIRCENSES AND THE POLITICS OF ENVY

In every major historic era, the diligent student of history will find epochal events and eerily familiar historic parallels. This is not because history is necessarily cyclical as many learned people believe, but because human nature itself has not changed in the last 6000 years of recorded history. Human nature and actions, particularly those of strong personalities, are responsible for many of the crucial human events recorded on its pages.

Consider the fact that in our own age, divisive political demagogues have honed down the politics of envy to a fine degree so that, for example, during the 1992-1994 debate, we repeatedly heard such terms as "price gouging" and "greedy providers," referring to the pharmaceutical industry and physicians, respectively—to instigate modern class warfare. And through 1995 and early 1996, we heard repeatedly the rhetorical mantra: "The Republicans are seeking to cut Medicare by $270 billion dollars to pay for a $245 billion dollar package of tax breaks for the rich."

This amplification of the divisive politics of envy has been employed to pave the way for the planned, step-by-step transformation of the American health care delivery system, and the subjugation of the medical profession as to make physicians employees of the up-and-coming, powerful private-public partnerships under the rubric of the oxymoron of managed competition and the statism of corporate socialized medicine.

To the student of history, the situation today becomes analogous to that which befell the Roman Republic in the 1st and 2nd Centuries B.C. For as you would remember—after nearly four centuries of glorious constitutional rule, triumphant conquests, and enormous expansion—the Roman Republic reached a pinnacle of prosperity and resplendence. It was then that it fell prey to populist demagogues who claimed to speak for the people and the lower classes, but spoke for their own selfish ends, their own greed, and their own thirst for power. They promised the populace land, bread, and circuses. They instigated riots and insurrections, and preached class hatred and class warfare in the name of justice and equality.

Law and order and the ancient Roman precept of the rule of law were discarded. For all intents and purposes, the once glorious Republic had degenerated into an unruly mass democracy, with populist politicians currying favor with the incited masses and threatening to establish a tyranny of the majority, a desultory majority which, no longer informed and vigilant, could be manipulated on the promise that they would be given other peoples' land and wealth. This chaotic situation could not stand, and it too, quickly degenerated into a mobocracy (the rule of the mob). Here we should perhaps pause and note the words of Sir Alex Fraser Tytler (18th Century): "A democracy cannot exist as a permanent form of government. It only exists until the voters discover they can vote themselves largess from the public treasury. From that moment on, the majority always votes for the candidates promising the most benefits from the public treasury, with the result that a democracy always collapses over loose fiscal policy, always followed by dictatorship. The average age of the world's great civilizations have been 200 years."

In the end, as is well known from history, when law and order disintegrate, the citizenry will inure oppression in exchange for peace and security; and in the end, give up their liberties and freedoms and hand power over to a strong man who promises to re-establish law and order. That is just what happened when Julius Caesar crossed the Rubicon, seized power in a bloody civil war, and formally overthrew the Republic. Roman citizens gave up their votes and their time-honored constitutional, republican principles happily, *quid pro quo*, public largesse and other *panem et circenses*. This included getting on the public dole for bread and other government subsidies, and being given free gladiatorial entertainment in the Roman arenas.

For their part, great men, statesmen, philosophers, and republican leaders like Cato the Younger, Cicero, and later, Seneca the Younger, died honorably for their republican sentiments and their beliefs in the natural rights of man, the rule of law, and the tenets of the Roman constitutional Republic.

Fortunately, as Terence once wrote, "Fortune favors the bold," and the mighty Roman Empire that followed and that enforced a *Pax Romana* for nearly two centuries, retained many of the republican institutions (such as the Consulate, the Roman Senate, and some of the rights of citizenship) so that even with the founding of a great empire, Rome, and by in large, the average Roman citizen, continued to prosper.

During this period, genuinely devoted medical ethicists and celebrated Roman physicians, such as Scribonius Largus and Aulus Celsus, flourished. Scribonius, for example, expounding on the precepts of Hippocrates, formulated the basic tenets of medical humanism, humanitarianism, patient responsibility for their own medical care, and prescribed the best possible drugs and medications for his patients. For his part, the Roman medicus, Celsus, took medicine to a pinnacle of glory in the fields of internal medicine, surgery, and professional ethics. And Pedacious Dioscorides, a Graeco-Roman surgeon who followed the Roman legions into far-reaching corners of the empire, expanded the frontiers of medical knowledge and wrote and illustrated his magnum opus on medical pharmacology, *De Materia Medica*.

All of these physicians believed in a sacrosanct patient-doctor relationship, and were able to place major building blocks of knowledge in the great edifice of medicine, because during this period, the practice of medicine remained independent and unimpeded by government intrusion. The practice of medicine was guided by virtue-based medical ethics and the sanctity of the patient-doctor relationship. Like Hippocrates' medical ethics, theirs was a voluntary, self-imposed, professional code. Medicine had become an honorable, respected, and learned profession. Wise governments recognized that physicians were valued members of a profession whose purpose and function ultimately benefitted society, and therefore, were best left alone to practice their profession, as long as they practiced according to the ethical standards of the particular school of philosophy to which they adhered and swore to uphold.

#### REFERENCES

1. Faria MA Jr. Vandals at the Gates of Medicine—Historic Perspectives on the Battle over Health Care Reform. Hacienda Publishing, Inc., Macon, Georgia, 1995.
2. Simkin J, Zelman A, and Rice AM. Lethal Laws. Milwaukee, Wisconsin, Jews for the Preservation of Firearms Ownership, 1994.
3. Olson WK. The Litigation Explosion—What Happened when America Unleashed the Lawsuit. Truman Talley Books, Dutton, New York, 1991.
4. McManus JF. Financial Terrorism—Highjacking America under the Threat of Bankruptcy. Western Island, Appleton, Wisconsin, 1993.
5. Barton D. The Myth of Separation. Wallbuilder Press, Aledo, Texas, 1991.
6. Faria MA Jr. The medical gulag. J Med Assoc Ga 1993;82(2):56. See Chapter 22.
7. Annis ER. Code Blue—Health Care in Crisis. Regnery Gateway, Washington, DC, 1993.

(NOVEMBER, 1994)

## CHAPTER 3

# *VANDALS WITHIN THE GATES*

All the information that has come to light regarding the deliberations, inappropriate and shocking revelations, of the secret Health Care Task Force of President Bill and First Lady Hillary Rodham Clinton thanks to the lawsuit, *AAPS v. Clinton*; and the subsequent wheeling and dealing behind closed doors of liberal democratic congressional leaders attempting to sugar-coat the Clintonian health care proposals (socialized medicine), remind me of the true story and the consequent sequence of historic events that led to the present situation concerning monetary and economic policies—e.g., an unstable weak currency, slow but chronic infla- tion, budget deficits, and ballooning national debt (now approaching $5 trillion)—and to the inception of an all-powerful monetary entity, the Federal Reserve System, which has been appropriately christened the "Creature from Jekyll Island" by G.E. Griffin in his magnificent exposé of the aforesaid name.[1]

Here is the shocking story: In the fall of 1910, a very secre- tive meeting was held on Jekyll Island, Georgia. The meeting was attended by a small cabal of banking elites who—many years later, after the fact—explained they had drafted a master plan to end the monopolistic practices of the New York bankers who controlled capital. Ostensibly, these individuals also wanted to stabilize the currency. What came out of the secret deliberations of these "reforming" banking elites (who represented one quarter of the wealth of the United States) was the blueprint for the Federal Reserve System which, unlike its name implied, proved to be neither federal, nor a reserve, nor a system.

It was, however, a private corporation and a quasi- government, hybrid entity with no inherent reserves of its own. And it was not even a system to decentralize power as its name suggested, but a veritable cartel—an agreement between competitors who sought to eliminate their competition and to implement a banking monopoly with control over the money supply, interest rates, and ultimately, the entire U.S. economy. Thus, this was not only a secret gentlemen's agreement by a handful of the well-connected and powerful people, but a veritable cabal operating against the public interest, and likely illegal, as the Sherman-Antitrust Act had been in effect since 1890.

The Federal Reserve Act, with all its ambiguous language, was hurriedly passed by Congress on December 22, 1913, so that, once secured in its passage, it could be worked and reworked to suit the pleasure of its creators: the Eastern banking establishment. Yet, during the time of debate over passage of this bill, this same establishment and many congressional leaders campaigned publicly against the Act to deceive the public as to its beneficiaries, not to mention the true intentions of this particular piece of legislation. You see, in a stroke of supreme duplicity, this same establishment had privately planned and engineered the provenance, declaration, and implementation of the Federal Reserve, with its ultimate goal not the decentralization of power of the big New York bankers, but rather the consolidation of their power in collusion and with the blessings of government. Thus, many authorities now believe that the true intention of this system was not necessarily to stabilize the currency and the banking system as proclaimed, but to create a government-approved cartel with a veritable monopoly over the money supply.[1]

Today, the Federal Reserve controls the printing of irredeemable (not backed by gold or silver) paper currency and therefore is capable of creating inflation at will. Yes, the creation of this fiat money is responsible for the steady decrease in the value of the currency and the persistent inflation to which we have become accustomed.[2] Inflation occurs, not as it is commonly believed (e.g., the result of higher prices for goods and services), but because there is more irredeemable paper money in circulation chasing relatively fewer goods and services. Inflation is, in effect, a hidden tax that affects all of us almost imperceptibly. The policies of the Federal Reserve not only cause the inflation that erodes the value of the currency (and the paycheck of hard-working Americans), but are also responsible for the stagflations (inflation accompanied by stagnant economic activity and high unemployment) and recessions that have periodically affected this country. It is also worth remembering, the Federal Reserve System presided over the decade-long, Great Depression that followed the Stock Market Crash of 1929, a depression this entity itself was supposed to forestall.

These historic events taken in the context of contemporary revelations gave me pause to wonder about the oxymoronic entity that emerged from Jackson Hole, Wyoming—*managed competition*. This is the much-touted health care option ostensibly created to control spiraling health care costs, but which in reality is leading day by day to the formation of an unholy partnership between the giant insurers and health care megacorporations, and big government—and the establishment of our own brand of socialized medicine, American style.

The centerpiece of managed competition is managed care, and whether this scheme utilizes any of the various appellations (i.e., purchasing cooperatives, regional alliances, or HMOs, PPOs, etc.), it amounts to nothing less than a government-approved cartel that favor big private entities poised to gain financial benefits under monopolistic government protection at the expense of small businesses, independent insurers, Mom and Pop local pharmacies, small entrepreneurs including physicians, and the public at large, particularly unwary patients.

It is imperative we recognize the fact that socialism today, in its preferred incarnation, *democratic socialism*, given the searing lesson of the unexpected collapse of the Soviet Empire, at least not openly seek government ownership of the means of production and distribution of goods and services, but merely, government control, regulation and taxation. Simply stated, with the alleged death of communism in the Soviet Union and Eastern Europe, even the most hardened collectivist has come to realize that central planning with control and regulation (Socialism) are far more effective (and efficient) than outright government ownership (Communism) of various sectors of the economy. And particularly in the case of health care, until the political winds change direction, it would be easier to deal with several behemothic megacorporations than with 600,000 independent-minded physicians, countless nurses and pharmacists, and a myriad of small indemnity insurers and entrepreneurs in the medical marketplace.

It is not surprising that the Health Care Task Force operated behind closed doors during the deliberations and drafting of the

Health Security Act of 1993. This pattern of willful machinations and secrecy are also reminiscent of the manipulations that gave rise to the "Creature from Jekyll Island."

As we teeter at the brink of the abyss of socialized medicine, we should question the intentions and motives of the big insurers and the megacorporations which pretended to oppose the Clinton plan during the heat of the great health care debate (1992-1994), but were (and are still) pushing for "Clinton-Lite" managed-competition reforms (at the national and particularly at the state level), even as I write these words—but are only just prevaricating. In reality, they are just asking for a little less of the same thing. This managed competition scheme has at its core plans for extensive networks of managed care and HMOs written not only by government bureaucrats, but as we now know, by individuals employed by private entities such as big foundations and allied health care networks that had (and have) a vested financial interest in seeing that managed care (preferably HMOs) is implemented as the centerpiece of the U.S. health care delivery system for the 1990s—and the 21st Century.

The lawsuit filed in 1993 by the Association of American Physicians and Surgeons (*AAPS v. Clinton*), disclosed that many special interests, who actively participated in the deliberations of the Health Care Task Force, wanted to profit by changing the American health care system, from fee-for-service to a pre-paid, managed competition option, more to their own liking and for their own financial benefit. This may well explain why private physicians were intentionally left out of the health care debate.

Likewise, the Federal Reserve Act was passed hurriedly in 1913 and then worked upon and reworked, until it suited the pleasure of the Eastern banking establishment that publicly had campaigned in opposition, while behind the scenes had engineered its creation and legislation. Once the Act was passed, the rest, as the saying goes, is history. One must stop here to ponder what former Democratic Senate Majority leader, George Mitchell of Maine, had in mind when, just before the November of 1994 epochal Congressional elections, he blurted, "Let us pass anything and we'll fix it in conference."

Things are not always what they seem, and at this critical juncture in the health care debate, physicians and their patients, and concerned citizens must remain alert, informed, and vigilant if they are, like St. George, to slay the multi-headed dragon of socialized medicine.

## A NEW DARK AGE

In the years A.D. 244-249, Roman Emperor Philip, "the Arab," planned a spectacular series of gladiatorial games and circuses galore to celebrate the 1000th anniversary of the founding of the Eternal City of Rome. He had proclaimed a "New Age." But this new age was not the new world order he envisioned, for the sun had begun to set on the declining Empire.

In fact, the Empire was being assailed by hordes of barbarians from outside her gates and plagued by domestic insurrections and civil wars from within. Rome suffered from decadence, anguish, and unremitting despair. The moral foundations on which the Roman Republic was founded had been greatly eroded. And as the scholar Michael Grant had proclaimed, it was a veritable "Age of Crisis." Emperors were murdered with impunity by their own rebellious troops or by treacherous imperial bodyguards. The Praetorian Guard seemed to possess the power to make or break emperors at will. For the first time in history, Roman emperors were killed or captured on the field of battle by the foreign invaders. The unthinkable was actually happening: Rome, the former mistress of the Mediterranean, was on the verge of total collapse.

Once again, as history has so often shown, in an instance of impending catastrophe, a great opportunity arouse in the year A.D. 284, when a strong man, the captain of the Imperial guard, Diocletian, rose to the occasion and was appointed Emperor. A powerful personality, Emperor Diocletian did not wait for prognosticated historic cycles, but proceeded to make history himself. And while his military genius is historically evident and indisputable, his political and economic policies were utter failures.[3]

Diocletian abolished the last vestiges of republican rule and established an autocratic system run by a gigantic bureaucracy to administer his new and visionary welfare state. And to pay for it, the currency was devalued and coins were minted in great numbers. Inflation, predictably, went unchecked and stringent wage and price controls were instituted in a futile attempt to check the same inflation and runaway prices the government itself had created. To get their "fair share" of government subsidies, farmers left their land and hurried to the crowded cities. Fields went unplowed. Common goods became scarce and had to be rationed. Prices soared. Black markets flourished. Riots broke out. Insurrections were ruthlessly crushed. A great opportunity had been lost when, after having secured the imperial borders and reestablished law and order, Diocletian had turned to totalitarianism rather than to the venerated republican institutions that had served Rome so well for so many centuries.

Throughout history, price controls during periods of high demand for goods and services have resulted in the scarcity of those same commodities and services. Draconian measures are then taken that result in arbitrary rationing, thriving black markets, and increased crime. Eventually, when price controls out of sheer necessity are lifted, prices rebound and soar out of the reach of the ordinary citizen. In the end, it's the very people a totalitarian government claims to protect that suffer the most.

So, it is not surprising that with the economic situation worsening, Diocletian passed draconian decrees making occupations, trades, and professions hereditary. A man was bound to his trade or occupation for life and so were his children. Failure to abide by these decrees were punishable by death.

At the same time, the largest and most ferocious persecution in history was carried out against Christians, in an attempt to eradicate Christianity, once and for all. Besides, distractions and convenient scapegoats were needed for the benefit of the new social and economic order.

With the vestiges of the constitutional republic explicitly abolished, the venerated, ancient Roman ideals—incarnated in the rule of law, the natural rights of man, social mobility, private property, and wealth creation—had all but been forgotten. A new despotism and totalitarianism replaced all of these noble Roman traditions. Swarms of officers and government agents, dependent on Diocletian's will and obstructing the administration of justice according to the precepts of the ancient Republic, travelled the countryside harassing the citizenry and enforcing authoritarian imperial decrees. The land was rife with magistrates, provincial officials, informers (and sundry whistle-blowers) who roamed the realm, spying on each other and sapping the substance of the people. Yet, even these ancient *apparatchiks* were themselves closely watched, for precautions were necessary to maintain the new order. Moreover, these "shared sacrifices" were necessary for the good of the state.

And, despite the harsh imperial decrees and penalties, stark inefficiencies, rampant fraud and abuse and bureaucratic corruption continued to plague the Empire, along with continued government infringements into every aspect of the lives of the people.

Physicians, like everybody else, became part of a trade, and were no longer bound to their revered Graeco-Roman medical ethics, but to the new "ethics" decreed by the state. For physicians, mere survival had become the order of the day. They no longer answered a calling. They did not serve their *individual* patients; they served the *state* or its surrogates. They practiced a trade highly regulated by the state bureaucracy and were bound to obey their new masters.

Medicine declined steadily, and centuries later, when the West was in the throes of the Dark Ages, the best medicine available, Byzantine medicine, as practiced in the enclave of Constantinople and in the Eastern Roman Empire, regressed to a lamentable and primitive state. Ethical medicine, as had been practiced centuries earlier under the great Graeco-Roman physicians: Hippocrates, Galen, Celsus, and Scribonius Largus—was only a semblance of its former self.

## At the Brink

All of the ingredients for the destruction of a civilization had, if fact, been added to the fatal brew. And less than two centuries later, the Eternal City of Rome (although by now Christianized) was sacked by Alaric and the Visigoths in A.D. 410, Gaiseric and the Vandals in A.D. 455, and finally completely overrun by sundry Germanic tribes led by King Odoacer in A.D. 476. In the West, the agonizing and regressive Dark Ages followed, while in the East, the Eastern Roman Empire centered in Constantinople held the barbarians at bay (by hook or by crook), enduring for another millennium.

Graeco-Roman medicine sank to its nadir. And in the 6th Century, still in the midst of the Dark Ages, the Great Plague assailed the known world mercilessly, ravaging the land and taking with it 100 million hapless victims. Miraculously, the remnants of Graeco-Roman medicine survived cloistered in the monasteries of the West in the form of monastic medicine, but the practice of private medicine would have to flourish elsewhere, and fortunately, resurgent it was, centuries later, in the Islamic countries.

Out of the ashes, medical schools and universities arose during the Medieval period. Then, during the Renaissance, medical care—under Paré, Paracelsus, and Vesalius—reached a new peak; and it flourished to full fruition in the scientific era of medicine, propelled by the genius of individual innovation and achievement, and aided by private philanthropy and the individual-based, free-enterprise system, during the late 19th and early 20th Centuries. It would reach a Golden Age in the post-World War II period.

The lessons of history sagaciously reveal wherever the government has sought to control medical care, medical practice and physicians (whether directly or indirectly), the results have been as perverse as they have been disastrous. In our own century, in the Soviet Union, in Nazi Germany, and in fascist Italy, medicine regressed and descended to unprecedented barbarism under the aegis of, or in partnership with, the state.

There is a renewed threat of a modern dark age looming on the medical horizon. It is the impending dark age of *corporate socialized medicine*, and if this form of industrial policy for health care is ever fully implemented in America, physicians and their patients can rest assured that they will be greatly affected. Physicians will find that they will be bound to obey new masters—the impersonal, faceless bureaucrats of the managed care megacorporations working under monopolistic government protection and whose motives are power and control, on the one hand; and corporate profits, on the other. For their part, patients will find that their new physicians dare not advise them what is best for them, but will do as they are told by the power-wielding bureaucrats of the third-party networks. Gone will be the independent-minded physicians of yore who took medicine to its pinnacle, free of government intrusion and coercion, who were able to treat their patients as individuals and place their patients' interest above their own, in the spirit of true altruism, philanthropy, and humanitarianism, and within the sanctity of the patient-doctor relationship.

The direction in which we are headed today in medicine is plain and simple—*corporate socialized medicine*—a concept centered around managed care/managed competition, gatekeepers, cost controls, and rationing, obfuscated by the profit motive and sanctioned by government authority. It employs bureaucrats who have a vested interest in preserving their positions of power and control and who dictate patient care from afar. The concept purports to rely on the false "ethics of caring," but in reality, is more akin to Professor Truffer's *veterinary ethics*, an ethic that forces physicians to act in the interest of the corporate entity as third-party payer, rather than in the interest of their patients;[4] it mandates coercive compassion, not true charity or philanthropy; it responds only to pressure by politically powerful special interests, not individual patient needs; and it insists on statism and collectivism, rather than individual self-interest and voluntary incentives.

For vigilant and informed citizens, there is no longer room on the sidelines. If we are not successful in our efforts, our fate will be the catastrophic stumble and inevitable plunge down the bottomless pit of *corporatism* and socialized medicine. This plunge would signify the commencement of a New Dark Age of medical care regression, health care rationing, and perhaps, in the not-too-distant future, a brave new world of government- or corporate-imposed, active euthanasia for the infirmed and elderly, the most vulnerable in our society—rationing by death—the ultimate and most efficient form of cost control.

You can be sure the responsibility for this debacle will be shouldered by the physicians, the healers, and not the politicians and bureaucrats; while the brunt of the cataclysm will be borne out by all of us consumers of medical care and ultimate patients. From the foregoing, it is obvious that this titanic conflict represents a political and moral struggle ordinary citizens of this great republic can not afford to lose. Let us remember Dante Alighieri's admonition: "The hottest place in Hell is reserved for those who in time of crisis profess their neutrality."

## REFERENCES

1. Griffin GE. The Creature from Jekyll Island. American Opinion Publishing, Inc.,

Appleton, Wisconsin, 1994.
2. Kudlow L. Fed up—the new gold standard. National Review 1994; 46(19): 51-54.
3. Faria MA Jr. Vandals at the Gates of Medicine—Historic Perspectives on the Battle Over Health Care Reform. Hacienda Publishing, Inc., Macon, Georgia, 1995, pp.133-137.
4. Ibid., pp.240-242.

(December, 1994)

## CHAPTER 4

# *CRISIS IN HEALTH CARE DELIVERY*

*In the late 1980s with the end of the Golden Age of Ronald Reagan and the early 1990s with the ascendancy of George Bush to the presidency, calls began to be heard about a looming "crisis" in health care delivery and solutions were proposed to reform the system. Three issues were widely identified by the mainstream media and the medical litera-ture as being responsible for the crisis: (1) soaring medical costs, (2) per-ceived high U.S. perinatal mortality statistics, and (3) the "growing" number of the uninsured needing universal coverage. I set out to discuss these issues in juxtaposition with the fully socialized health care systems that we find today in Great Britain and Canada—health care systems which are beginning to unravel under the pressure of increasing costs and government inefficiency, infinite demand, limited resources, and unbearable taxation.*

*Moreover, I brought to the forefront two other issues I posited (and still believe) to be the true culprits behind the real "crisis"—(4) the medical liability crisis, and (5) growing government intrusion into the medical arena which increasingly foments mutual mistrust in the patient-doctor relationship and has led to the develop-ment of a siege mentality among practitioners, a mentality which, by the early 1990s, had culminated in countless physicians leaving the profes-sion, and for the first time ever, advising their children not to follow in their footsteps into the medical field.*

### RESCUING MEDICINE FROM THE CLUTCHES OF GOVERNMENT

A recent AAPS bulletin brings to light the government assault on the medical profession with the use of administrative (unconstitutional) law applied against physicians charged (not con-victed) with medical fraud, so that their assets (i.e., home, cars, offices) could be confiscated during investigative proceedings (e.g., Medicare reimbursement disputes or sanctions).[1]

It is time for physicians to counterattack in the battle for the best health care for our citizens and to rescue our profession from the clutches of government intervention. Otherwise, our adver-saries and detractors will use real and/or perceived weaknesses in

our health care system as an excuse to push us further into socialized medicine.

We have become overly dependent on government while
making an infinite demand for medical services and technology. We
have paid for our false expectations by allowing government to
intrude in all aspects of our lives, including American medicine.
Now government intrusion with interference in the patient-doctor
relationship continues relentlessly in our bumpy ride toward full-
scale socialized medicine.

With this background in mind, I will now briefly address
those critical issues and discuss a promising set of solutions which
are derived in part by proposals from at least two respected
conservative think tanks, proposals which have been made public
yet have not been adequately or sufficiently explored by the policymakers, especially those who have the unqualified attention of the
mass media.

We should militate for discussion of these health care issues
because they are important. We as physicians have a singular
responsibility in rescuing medicine, because if we don't, then
others, who do not have the best interest of our profession at heart,
will try to do it for us, not only to our detriment, but to that of our
patients.

## SOARING MEDICAL COSTS

Perhaps, the first issue of contention in the health care
debate is spiraling health care costs, not quality as one would
expect given the paradoxical medical liability crisis that engulfs
practicing physicians, particularly those in high-risk specialties (e.g.,
obstetrics, orthopedics, neurosurgery, etc.). By 1996, we will be
spending nearly one trillion dollars (compared to $750 billion in
1992) on health care, including both private and public spending.

There are several reasons for high medical costs, and fore-
most among these are the recent proliferation of expensive medical
technology, the expense of research and development of drugs,
utilization and overutilization of medical services by a health-
minded citizens as well as an increasing aging population, and
*defensive medicine* as a direct consequence of the medical liability
crisis. For one thing, it is no providential revelation Americans have

become dependent on government for security in various aspects of their lives and thus have come to expect infinite access to services. This includes medical services as well as highly expensive technology. The tendency toward socialization of American medicine that began in 1965 with the Medicare Act has not only led to false security, but has resulted in growing inefficiency, entangling red tape, burgeoning bureaucracy, and interference in the sacrosanct patient-doctor relationship. The more money thrown upon the flames, the more blazing and glaring burn the consuming fire of government profligacy—and paradoxically, the more calls for social-ization, i.e., Medicare, Medicaid, managed care, Diagnostic Related Groups (DRGs), Resource-Based Relative Value Scales (RBRVS), and most recently, managed competition.

Total health care costs are increasing at a rate of 10% per year which, not surprisingly, parallels government domestic spending and contributes to the mindboggling U.S. record deficits unsurpassed in history, now nearing $5 trillion. Not surprisingly (at least to those familiar with the free-market), in the last two years government-run medical care (i.e., Medicare and Medicaid) has outpaced spending in the private sector. Be that as it may, by the year 2000, the projected cost of health care will more than top $1 trillion!

A crucial issue contributing to skyrocketing health care costs and needing open discussion is the problem of unhealthy lifestyles and the living-on-the-edge self-destructive behaviors that are the norm for many Americans. In a pungent editorial, Timothy Norbeck, Executive Director of the Connecticut Medical Association, opined that self-destructive and abusive American lifestyles promote poor health and disease. He wrote, "It seems the wise old adage 'an ounce of prevention is worth a pound of cure' has gone down the drain."[2] Despite the paradox of the punishment we inflict upon ourselves by these self-indulgent lifestyles, when the time of serious disease, age-related infirmity, or even terminal condi-tions arrive, we cling tenaciously to life at any price. And yes, an astounding 80% of illnesses can be linked to smoking, alcohol con-sumption, illicit drugs, poor diet, obesity, or sexual promiscuity. And it's not just the old that account for the fact that 4% of the people in the U.S. consume 55% of *all* hospital costs.

Near the end of life: 25-35% of Medicare funds are spent on 5-6% of enrollees who die within a year, and 85% of an individual's health care expenses occur in the last two years of life.

At the other end of the spectrum, American children are becoming more sedentary, and as a result, there is evidence 40% of children ages 5-8 are at risk of developing heart disease prematurely. Despite all the media hype about fitness and health fads, yuppies and other adults who have been advised to participate in cardiovascular fitness, vigorous 20-minute exercises three times a week, respond with a paltry 8%, far below the expected 60% compliance rate. Americans continue to consume too much fat and cholesterol, too much sugar and salt, and not enough fruits, vegetables, fiber, and grain products. Moreover, 1100 people die *daily* as a result of chronic tobacco use, despite the various warnings of the Surgeon General and the take-no-prisoners war against the tobacco industry.

"These same Americans," says Norbeck, "have a fierce desire to live as long as possible—the cost be damned"; meanwhile, the doctor, hospital, and health care system are blamed for high health care costs! In fact, a whopping 1/3 of all health care costs is *directly* attributed to self-abusive and destructive lifestyles beyond the purview of medicine. Increased longevity and improved quality of life could therefore be accomplished by paying attention to dieting, exercising, and ceasing smoking while at the same time cutting down health care costs.

Finally, despite media hype, physicians' fees as a proportion of total health care expenditures have remained frozen at 19% since 1950. Moreover, for 7 of the last 10 years, physicians' fees have not even kept pace with inflation. Physicians' fees are only a small portion of soaring medical costs.

### HIGH PERINATAL MORTALITY

Another perceived and frequently cited problem in the American health care system is *high perinatal mortality* in the U.S. as compared to other industrialized countries. The truth of the matter is that when compared to other industrialized nations, at any given high-risk birth weight, perinatal survival in the United States is substantially higher than that in any other industrialized country, including Japan and Norway, which tout the lowest overall infant mortality rates in the world.[3]

The problem in the United States is that we have a high percentage of low-birth weight and premature babies. Many of these unfortunate babies are born in a milieu of teenage sex, drug addiction, illiteracy, alcoholism, sexually-transmitted diseases, insufficient or total lack of prenatal care (even when widely available via Medicaid), unhealthy lifestyles (i.e., there is evidence the majority of teenage women who smoke continue to do so during pregnancy).

Single parenthood, teenage pregnancy, and smoking have all been definitely linked to increased risk of prematurity and low birth weight babies, conditions which are more prevalent in the U.S. than in other industrialized countries such as Canada, Japan, and Norway. Yet, these socioeconomic problems are only marginally-related to medical practice and even less to quality medical care. It is with good reason Dr. Henry Lerner argues that "sick and premature babies receive better care in the United States than in any other place in the world."[4]

### THE UNINSURED

The third and perhaps most pressing problem is that of the *plight of the much talked about 34-37 million Americans who are uninsured and underinsured.* This is the number of people who are actually uninsured for any given one month period either because of lack of affordability or portability of health insurance. Sixty percent of them are working adults and their families.[5]

Yet, the fact is that *only 4% of the population lacks health insurance for 2 years of longer.*[6] There is a national consensus these people should not be forgotten and should be taken care of by society. So here I would like to discuss the basis for extending coverage and providing the means of access to everyone. Probing deeply, one finds in the last decade, paradoxically, while the majority of the American public is willing to extend coverage to all in our society, when questioned further, less than a third are willing to foot the bill. It's also noteworthy that the public (70%) believes that any health care initiative must be associated with incentives for people to work.[7] Seventeen percent of the uninsured and underinsured are unemployed, the other 57% are self-employed or employed in small businesses that do not provide insurance coverage.* The rest are dependent children or those who are self-employed.[5] Our long-term goals should not only be to preserve, and to improve quality, and make health care more cost effective, but also to improve access for all Americans.

One final point that should be mentioned here is that while one hears and reads much about physicians' income in the media, little attention is given to the charity or uncompensated care provided by American physicians. For instance, a recent AMA survey showed American physicians provide $11 billion of uncompensated care (or an average of 150 hours of care annually free of charge).[8] Specifically, data from California shows that $50,000 of uncompensated care is provided per physician either *pro bono publico* or governmentally mandated.

## THE MEDICAL LIABILITY CRISIS

The unrealistically high (and sometimes false) expectations of the American public as to the degree of care physicians and modern medicine can provide is intricately related to the climate that has fostered the defensive medicine practiced by a large segment of American physicians, and to the medical liability crisis that threatens our nation. It's no secret as a result of the adversarial, litigious climate in which medicine is practiced today, $60 billion is spent annually in defensive medicine unnecessarily. Moreover, our society spends $300 billion annually in litigation of all types, at least one-third of which, is deemed frivolous.[9]

Furthermore, a myth that needs debunking is that litigation weeds out the "bad doctors." The fact is that it's not the bad doctors who most frequently get sued but the physicians who treat the sickest patients and who require the use of high-risk procedures and advanced technology that accrue to the various specialties. Unfortunately, since medicine is still an inexact science and sometimes things don't quite go as planned, a lawsuit is the result. Today, 20% of a physician's overhead is consumed in medical liability

*These individuals would be given a great incentive for obtaining their own insurance coverage if they were allowed to establish their own tax-free, medical savings accounts.

premiums. Moreover, litigation per se is a major cause of increasing health care costs. For example, automobile accident victims who hire a lawyer "run up three times the medical expenses of people who don't."[9]

Much has been said about the Canadian health care system. The fact is Canadian patients sue their doctors much less than Americans sue theirs—even though Canadian physicians do not practice better medicine than their American counterparts.

Moreover, their legal system has disincentives for medical litigation (i.e., plaintiff attorneys pay court costs when they lose in court; contingency fees are prohibited in some provinces such as Ontario; punitive damages are rare; and there is a cap on non-economic damages). The result is that Canadian physicians get sued only 20% as much as U.S. physicians, and they pay only one-tenth of U.S. malpractice premiums.[10] To their credit, the AMA's "Health Access America" and President Bush's "Health Care Plan" include malpractice tort reform in their respective packages.

Yet, given this destructive litigation climate, I seriously believe that no plan, no matter how elegant and comprehensive, will solve the health care crisis unless medical liability tort reform is instituted as part of its overall package. The fact is the litigation explosion has unleashed a destructive juggernaut which is unravelling the very fabric of our society and is now threatening to undermine our health care delivery system.

## SOCIALIZED VS. "PRIVATE" MEDICINE

In contrast to what we may have been led to believe, our medical care system is already socialized. For instance, in Canada, 74% of all health care expenditures are in the government sector. In the United States, it is already 42%. The debate, therefore, has implicitly centered on the degree of government intrusion and control of American medicine using the expedient excuse of bringing down health care costs. Nevertheless, when adjustments are made for inflation and the fact the Canadian economy has grown faster than the American economy in the last 20 years, as well as the fact that the Canadian population is younger and has different demographics, and one further considers the fact that long-term health care is not included in Canadian statistics, *Canadian health care expenditures equal U.S. expenditures.*[10] Canadian health care, on a per capita basis and adjusted for inflation, rose at an average annual rate of 4.58% compared to 4.38% in the United States. If anything, it is slightly higher than in the U.S. This is true even when Canada lags behind the U.S. in research, development, and medical technology.[10]

We must not lose sight of the fact that we have the best health care and the best medical technology in the world and should learn from studying its strengths as well as its weaknesses. The truth of this statement is self-evident, especially when the inescapable comparison is made with the socialized systems of health care elsewhere. It then quickly becomes obvious that while we continue to improve quality, socialized countries are stalled or pulling back from research and development, while simultaneously reducing access via waiting lists, reduction of services, and overt rationing.

If a Canadian styled public health insurance program were to be implemented in the United States, it would cost conservatively anywhere between $250-$500 billion annually *in added* health care expenditures. According to the Dallas-based National Center for Policy Analysis,[11] whether this gargantuan expenditure is funded by a payroll tax or through income taxing, the tax rate increase will be on the average 14%. If one opted for a consumption tax, the price of every food and commodity will be expected to rise 10% relative to income (as it did in Canada). If funded by the payroll tax, the tax rate will rise from its current level of 15% to a rate of 29%.

Interestingly, National Public Radio (NPR) on April 9, 1992 reported that record numbers of Canadians were crossing the border to buy goods and commodities such as milk, bread, and gasoline in the United States, because they are 25-50% cheaper here. Why? Several reasons, but most prominently, the media pundits admitted, was the high sales tax Canadians pay to support the much touted Canadian health care system. Canadians pay 55% in federal and provincial income taxes and an additional 15% sales tax on all items for a total taxation of 70%. In other words, Canadians work for the government through mid-August each year before it's time for take-home pay.

One should not lose sight of the fact that social democracies have lower health care costs by limiting available services, including spending limits and curtailing access to specialists. They also reduce utilization of available services by horrendous *waiting lists*, *queues*, and outright health care *rationing*. For example, in Britain during 1978, "33% of the dialysis centers refused to treat patients over the age of 55." Today, there are 800,000 patients waiting for surgery in Great Britain.[10] In Canada, "the risk of waiting for heart surgery now exceeds the danger of dying on the operating table."[12] In Toronto alone, there are an estimated 1,000 people waiting longer than a year for coronary bypass surgery. Many are coming across the border to the United States to get their bypass surgery performed sooner. In Sweden, citizens pay 60% of their wages in taxes and wait in long lines for "free" medical care such as cataract operations, hip replacements, and heart bypass surgery.[10]

To be fair to the Canadian situation, one should concede two advantages they have over us. The first I have previously mentioned, and that is the much lower rate of medical (malpractice) litigation. The other is that 70% of Canadian physicians are in primary care and individuals in general tend to form a more trusting and lasting patient-doctor relationship with physicians whom they see repeatedly. In the United States, our more technologically-prone society is the reverse: 70% specialists versus 30% primary care physicians.

As alluded to earlier, American medicine by many parameters today could be considered already socialized, i.e., government control via the RBRVS, DRGs, Medicare and Medicaid, extrapolation of data and statistics to intimidate physicians accepting government payments in Medicare disputes, together with the frequent use of threats in the sanctioning process of quality and utilization reviews—all of which have made medicine lose its luster. I don't have to remind the reader by whatever parameter we use—except for our calling, our inherent need to treat the ill and afflicted— dissatisfaction is rampant in the medical profession today.[1,3,13]

What separates us from total socialization and total control is the fact we have multiple third-party payers. *Socialized medicine* has come to mean a single-payer system—the government—and it goes by the innocuous name of *National Health Insurance*. But multiple third-party payers will not prevent the further socialization of American medicine. Thus, I agree with the the the AMA *pronunci-amiento* that government does have a role in health care:To provide a formula *utilizing the private sector to promote universal access* at competitive affordable costs while preserving quality health care.[8] It is obvious this formula is the promotion of individually-owned, tax-free MSAs coupled with high-deductible, catastrophic insurance coverage as advanced by the Association of American Physicians and Surgeons (AAPS).

### THE SOLUTION

It is ironic that while other countries are moving away from Marxist ideology, we in the United States continue to march, in evolutionary fashion, to the drumbeat of socialist policies in health care, despite the obvious failure of government interference in medicine. It should be noted that despite a steady barrage of unfavorable publicity, our health care takes care of 87% of all Americans (who are fully insured) and two-thirds of these, are satisfied with their health care.[8] We must also remember that over 50% of the Nobel Peace prizes awarded in Medicine and Physiology have been won by Americans.

Yet, calls for the dismantling of our system are being heard from all quarters.The battering rams are pounding at the gates with the result that the status quo will not be allowed to stand. We can make a good situation out of a potentially catastrophic one. We should revamp the U.S. health care system by removing outright the omnipresent government regulations, thereby freeing physicians to do what they do best, take care of their individual patients, and rescuing medicine from the clutches of government.

Toward this goal, Dr. Robert Moffit, of The Heritage Foundation, and Dr. John C. Goodman, of the National Center for Policy Analysis have proposed *consumer-oriented free-market approaches* to health care which deserve serious consideration.[11,14,15]

I have borrowed from these innovative proposals which encourage individual choice and responsibility in my discussion of "the solution." A *voucher* system may be used for patients who cannot afford health insurance and *refundable tax credits* for those who can. M*edical Savings Accounts* ("Medisave"), should be created in which money can be put aside for routine medical care costs, tax free, and out of the reach of government. The Medisave coupled with high-deductible insurance, which can be used for truly catastrophic illnesses, major surgery, or when the deductible has been satisfied would be the backbone of the program. High-deductible insurance for catastrophic coverage will be available to individuals at competitive and affordable rates with premiums paid from savings in the Medisave account or from the tax credits or vouchers.

Americans would then have the incentive to conserve because they would be allowed to keep the money they do not spend in the Medisave account (it can only be used for medical reasons, or alternatively, it can be rolled into a pension fund). Thus patients would use truly free-market techniques to control costs (as they do with everything else when they act as consumers) while at the same time being in charge of their own health care. Everyone would have the incentive and the means to provide for their health care, free of governmental interference.

The bedrock of the system is that it preserves patient choice of physicians and the trust inherent in the individually-based, patient-doctor relationship, while restoring patient and physician autonomy.

I will add that insurance and medical liability tort reform will be imperative if this plan is to succeed. Likewise, medical ethics and true compassionate care will also be given a new impetus to maintain the high standards of the profession.

Therefore, I propose we refer to this system as the *patient-oriented, free-market approach* to medical care when it is coupled with a reinvigoration of medical (Hippocratic) ethics and the virtues of the compassionate, honorable physicians, as well as meaningful medical liability tort reform. Historic precedent establishes no inconsistency in a marriage between free-market principles and ethical compassionate care.[16]

I urge all physicians to be well-informed and involved in organized medicine. The health care of our patients now, and that of our children in the future, are at stake. Let us stand up and be counted for the restoration of the principles of our noble profession which can only be accomplished by stemming the *red* tidal wave of government control and over-regulation in medicine. Let us be aggressive in striving for the *patient-oriented, free-market approach* to health care before it's too late.

### REFERENCES

1. AAPS News Bulletin, May 1992. AAPS, 1601 N. Tucson, Blvd., Suite 9, Tucson, Arizona 85716. 800-635-1196.
2. Norbeck TB. Telling the truth about rising health care costs. Private Practice, February 1990.
3. AAPS News Bulletin (Supplement), March and April 1992. AAPS, 1601 N. Tucson Blvd., Suite 9, Tucson, Arizona 85716.
4. Lerner H. Private Practice, August 1990.
5. American Medical Association. Advocacy Briefs. October 1991.
6. Swartz and McBride. Spells without health insurance: distributions or durations and their link to the point-in time estimates of the uninsured. Blue Cross Blue Shield, Fall 1990. Cited by MD Tanner in, Individual medical accounts, a consumer oriented health proposal. Georgia Public Policy Foundation, May 1992.
7. Blendon RJ. What should be done about the universal poor? JAMA 1988;260:3176-3177.
8. American Medical Association. Health Access America. November 1991, p. 1-15.
9. Olson W. The Litigation Explosion—What Happened When America Unleashed the Lawsuit. Truman-Talley Books, Dutton, New York, 1991.
10. Lee RW. Free Medicine. The New American, 1991. The New American, P.O. Box 8040, Appleton, WI. 54913.
11. Goodman JC. An Agenda for Solving America's Health Care Crisis, 1991. National Center for Policy Analysis, 12655 North Central Expressway, Suite 720, Dallas, Tx. 75243. (214) 386-6276.
12. Tanner MD. Commentary. Georgia Public Policy Foundation. February 10, 1992.
13. Faria MA Jr. Enemies of private practice bide their time. Private Practice 1992;24:33-34.
14. Moffit R. Comparable Worth for Doctors: A Severe Case of Government Malpractice. 1991. The Heritage Foundation, 214 Massachusetts Ave. N.E., Washington, D.C. 20002. (202) 546-4400.
15. Moffit R. Consumer Choice in Health: Learning From The Federal Employee Health Benefits Program, 1992. The Heritage Foundation, 214 Massachusetts Ave., N.E., Washington, D.C. 20002. (202) 546-4400.
16. Faria MA Jr. The Forging of the Renaissance Physician (Parts I-IV) J Med Assoc Ga, March and April, 1992.

(NOVEMBER, 1992)

# PART TWO: MEDICAL ECOLOGY

## Chapter 5

# ON ENVIRONMENTALISM, RADICALISM PREVAILS

*...The last chance for a future that makes ecological sense...We thought that the one-month deadline for the writing [of this Manifesto] was impossible, that we could easily spend a year on it. But a year is about one-fifth of the time that we have left if we are going to preserve any kind of quality in our world.*

> The Environmental Handbook, Earth Day celebration, 1970. Quoted 22 years later by Gary Benoit, editor of *The New American*, June 1, 1992.

We all want clean air, clean water, and a clean environment. And, indeed, true environmental problems abound. One only has to discern the ecological disaster brought about by the totalitarian Marxist regimes of Eastern and Central Europe over years of environmental degradation and senseless central planning: industrial air and water pollution, improper waste disposal, deforestation, even water depletion of natural water reservoirs, e.g., lakes. In fact, the fourth largest lake (the Aral Sea in the former USSR) has been largely dried up and the adjacent land turned into a wasteland from irresponsible drainage and over-irrigation. Then, there was the disastrous 1986 incident at Chernobyl, the most serious nuclear accident on record. As you would remember, the outdated Soviet reactor's cooling system failed, the nuclear core overheated, and fire resulted.[1] The nuclear fall-out that ensued resulted in extensive nuclear contamination throughout Eastern Europe, particularly the Ukraine, and Scandinavia. The tragedy incurred a heavy toll on human lives and resources. In short, the fact is the worse environmental calamities have taken place in socialists states where authoritative, heavy handed, government bureaucrats regulate, control, and dictate environmental policies.

With the fall of the Berlin Wall in 1989 and the collapse of the Soviet Union in 1991, the revelations coming from behind the Iron Curtain confirm government control and regulation of the environment has resulted in environmental degradation, plundering of habitats, and ecosystems destruction, as a rule rather than an exception. This should by no means be surprising. Individuals in a free society pursuing their own self-interest take better care of their environment than their *apparatchik* counterparts pursuing state interests. Individuals who have a vested interest in the conservation of their private resources (be it land or habitats) do a better job than an impersonal bureaucracy whose main interest is self-preservation and the exercise of regulatory power.

While I do believe we have legitimate ecologic and environmental problems that deserve our attention (e.g., endangered flora and fauna species; deforestation; wanton destruction of habitats; overpopulation, especially in Third World countries such as India and Pakistan)—I do believe that the looming apocalyptic prophecies have been greatly exaggerated. It seems that zealous environmentalists, cheered by the media, have effectively silenced many scientists and honest researchers who do not share their views. So, contrary views, such as those espoused by prominent scientists like Dr. Edward C. Krug, an environmental scientist formerly with the U.S. National Acid Rain Precipitation Assessment Program (NAPAP), and Dr. Elizabeth Whelan, President of the American Council on Science and Health, are seldom given a forum *a la par* afforded to those who toe the politically correct environmental line.

While some environmentalists like Paul Ehrlich subscribe to an exaggerated, distorted version of Malthusian environmental economics, namely that poverty and hunger increase faster than the means of subsistence, and therefore, that population has to be drastically controlled, the vast majority of economists today including a number of Nobel Prize winners believe that technology and modern agriculture can cope with predicted population growth. As Krug points out:"By 1985 agricultural surpluses became so vast that in the five years that followed, of some 300 million acres of U.S. farmlands, 60 million were taken out of production—30 million under the conservation reserve program. Nearly half of that land is reverting to national uplands and wetlands."[2]

In the environmental bandwagon, as far as publicity, the same fringe wheel gets all the grease. Instead of the public trusting the opinions of objective scientists, it seems it is the radical fringe of environmentalists who influence public opinion and thereby public policy. Consider the results of a survey reported by *The Washington Times* (August 1990): "[1] Only 15% of the American public trusts what government scientists say. [2] Only 6% trust scientists seen as representing industry. [3] 68% implicitly believe political activists. [4] 67% agree with the statement:'Threats to the environment are as serious as environmental groups say they are.' "[2] As a result of media hype and environmental extremism, both private and public sector scientists have been censored from the debate.

With good reason Krug believes that the environmental political ethics are ruinous for ecological systems because they divert attention from the real environmental concerns which although more serious are less publicized. He believes that the strident environmentalists are more interested in social engineering and political power than in genuine environmental problems. In another classic paper in *Imprimis* he cites real problems that have been poorly addressed:

(1) The elm trees dying, "not from acid rain or air pollution but from Dutch elm disease."

(2) The eastern hardwood forests (approx. 150 million acres) being decimated by imported diseases and pests (e.g., chestnut blight; oak which was replacing elms and chestnuts decimated by gypsy moths; beech by beech bark disease from Canada; 18 million acres of spruce-fir forests devastated by imported insect pests like the woolly adelgid, etc.).

(3) The zebra mussel introduced in 1986 from Norway destroying our aquatic ecosystem. Without natural enemies it has spread in American lakes feeding on the planktonic base sustenance of the food chain taking over 100 million acres of high-productivity freshwater lakes and causing danger to water supply systems and industry. Krug writes:

*If the Environmental Party were a genuine champion of the environment, it would not be preoccupied with multi-billion dollar acid rain controls or its other pet concerns like the spotted owl and the snail darter. It would not embrace nominal environmental issues that are used to acquire control over vital industrial activities and it would not ignore greater environmental problems just because they cannot be used to achieve such control.*

   *The truth is that the Environmental Party is dominated
by false prophets whose concern for the environment masks their
real agenda, which is social engineering, and their ultimate goal,
which is power.*[3]

## ACID RAIN/ACIDIC LAKES

   Despite the findings of the multimillion dollar National Acid
Precipitation Assessment Program, which called into question many
of the accepted claims of impending disaster, Congress went on to
enact and President Bush to sign, costly provisions (estimated at $40
billion annually) to neutralize acid rain in the Clean Air Act of 1990.
Many of these provisions such as those purported to combat the
acidity of northeastern lakes were totally unnecessary.

## DEFORESTATION

   Deforestation is taking place in the Eastern U.S. as a result
of insects and imported pests and diseases rather than urban
destruction. Moreover, private forest management in the U.S. in
terms of forest expansion outpaces federally managed preserves
because of private replanting and conservation efforts. From 1952 to
1987, there has been a 24% increase in forest growth. Most of this
increase has taken place in the forests of the North and South where
private ownership ranges from 80% to 90%, rather than in the
federally owned Western forests.[4] Because of man's nature to protect
his own, private property owners turn out to be better stewards of
the land than armchair bureaucrats trying to micromanage the
environment.

## AIR POLLUTION

   As Dr. Dixie Lee Ray pointed out in her book, "all of the air
polluting material produced by man since the beginning of the
industrial revolution do not begin to equal the quantities of toxic
material, aerosols, and particles spewed into the air from just three
volcanoes: Krakatoa in Indonesia in 1883, Mount Katsrai Alaska in

1912, and Hekla in Iceland in 1947."[5] To this list, Robert W. Lee adds: Mount St. Helens in Washington (1980) which effused 910 metric tons of carbon dioxide alone, El Chicon in Mexico (1982) which emitted 100 million tons of sulfur gases (and scoured the priceless Mayan ruins of Palenque), and Mount Pinatubo in the Philippines which blew off 30 million tons of pollutants into the stratosphere.[6]

### GLOBAL WARMING

The emission of carbon dioxide and other "greenhouse" gases has been blamed for the impending cataclysm of global warming, which until recently (and not helped by this season's winter arctic weather) was one of the most frightening of environmental stories. The fact is that in the last 50 years global mean temperature has risen only by a mere 1/2 degree Celsius and there is no recorded trend of long-term increases or decreases in the last 10,000 years, since the time of the last Ice Age. Thus, there's no credible scientific evidence that the Earth is either heating or cooling. And although carbon dioxide levels have indeed risen (without a concomitant increase in temperature), legions of scientists have considered this elevation in carbon dioxide levels to be potentially a boon for mankind because of its beneficial effects on plant growth via the process of photosynthesis.[7]

Behind the facade of fighting air pollution and global warming, stands the reality of government expansion, increasing taxation and regulation, and wealth redistribution. In fact, the big thrust of the Earth Summit (1992) was to find ways to levy huge taxes for the burning of fossil fuels (the Carbon [C] tax) on citizens of industrialized nations and to transfer the proceeds via the United Nations to the governments of undeveloped countries. Were the radical agenda of the environmental lobby enacted, the result could be devastating (i.e., doubling the prices of gasoline and electricity as a starter), increased taxation, and regulatory overkill.[47]

### WETLANDS/CRITICAL HABITATS

You will be surprised to learn the federal government

already owns more than one third of the land in the United States. And each year the U.S. appropriates millions of dollars in land acquisition projects—some acquisitions take place whether the citizens surrender their land (and sometimes their homes) voluntarily or not. More and more of this land, then, becomes off-limits to the public and closed for development. "One out of every eight acres the U.S. government owns—is designated as wilderness areas where 'the hand of man is not allowed to set foot.' "[7]

Two developments in the last 20 years have made it easier for the federal government to satiate its voracious appetite for peoples' land and private property: The Endangered Species Act of 1973 and The Clean Water Act of 1972—both derived from "the public trust doctrine"—which in effect circumvents traditional, constitutionally-protected private property rights. The former has resulted in the "listing" of the spotted owl as a threatened species and the consequent unemployment of hundreds of timber industry residents in Oregon, Washington, and California and the designation of millions of acres in the region as "critical habitat." Almost daily, more and more private land is set aside because of sightings of the bird which is essentially ubiquitous in the region. These sightings, in turn, translate to autocratic checks on private development in the region.[7]

The appellation of wetlands has provided another readily available pretext for government regulatory taking and violation of private property rights. With the use of administrative law, asset forfeiture statues, and the designation of a "wetland" to private property, the constitutional rights to liberty and property have been trampled upon by government authorities. The designation of a citizen's private property as a wetland entails, for all intent and purposes, "a taking" of private property rights by the government. And what, after all, defines a wetland? According to the Wetlands Delineation Manual published in 1989 by the EPA and the U.S. Army Corps of Engineers: The presence of water 18 inches below ground for 7 consecutive days out of the year.[*]

Criminal prosecution is also utilized to enforce strict

---

[*] The U.S. Army Corps of Engineers, more recently, has also designated "wetlands" any land property with the mere growth of such common vegetation as "skunk cabbage and sweet gum trees."[7]

compliance, as Pennsylvania mechanic John Poszgai found out when he cleared off some rubbish-filled land and filled his "wetland" with dirt[7]—he is in prison serving a 3-year term.*

We should all be for clean air, clean water, preservation of forests and pristine habitats, whether wetlands or dry-lands, but as things now stand, the pendulum has swung too far to the left on most eco-environmental issues. Science should prevail over eco-extremism. Let us be informed and militate for the voice of reason and moderation to prevail in this critically important issue involving Mother Nature.

### REFERENCES

1. The Columbia Encyclopedia. Franklin Electronic Publishers Inc.    Columbia University Press 1989.
2. Krug EC. The real green revolution. St. Louis-Dispatch, May 7, 1993.
3. Krug EC. Save the planet, sacrifice the people—the environmental party's bid for power. Imprimis 1991;20(7):1-5.
4. Lee RW. Lungs of the earth. The New American 1992;8(11):13. (Special Issue—The Resilient Earth. Reprints available from University Microfilms [1-800-521-0600]).
5. Ray DL, Guzzo L. Trashing the Planet. Harper Perennial 1992.
6. Lee RW. Fury of mother nature. The New American 1992;8(11):5.
7. Wrabek T. They are after your property. The New American, op. cit., pp. 23-24.
8. Rice CE. Net loss of freedom. The New American, op. cit., p. 29.

(MAY, 1994)

---

* Poszgai was actually convicted of violating the Clean Water Act. A humble Hungarian immigrant (from the 1956 uprising), Poszgai, had a gross income of approximately $20,000 a year and no assets, yet was also fined "an assessment" of $202,000 for his temerity and incurring the wrath of an environmental judge![8]

# PART THREE: TOWARDS COLLECTIVISM IN MEDICINE

51

CHAPTER 6

# CHILD ABUSE AND THE BREAKDOWN OF THE FAMILY

*The ideal for which the family stands is liberty. It is the only institution that is at once necessary and voluntary. It is the only check on the state that is bound to renew itself as eternally as the state, and more naturally than the state.*

G.K. Chesterton (1874-1936)

*When families fail, society fails. The anarchy and lack of structure in our inner cities are testament to how quickly civilization falls apart when the family foundation cracks. Children need love and discipline. They need mother and father. It is from parents that children learn how to believe in society....Among families headed by married couples today, there is a poverty rate of 5.7%. But 33.4% of families headed by a single mother are in poverty today....It doesn't help matters when prime time TV has Murphy Brown—a character who supposedly epitomizes today's intelligent, highly paid, professional woman—mocking the importance of fathers, by bearing a child alone, and calling it just another "lifestyle choice"....It's time to talk again about family, hard work, integrity, and personal responsibility.*

Vice President Dan Quayle
San Francisco, May 19, 1992

An unsavory but very important cultural war that can not be ignored by physicians is currently being waged in America. The battlelines of this war have been drawn almost incipiently, as if not wanting to arouse the rest of us. The ostensible cause of this war is the most repugnant and egregious crime, that of alleged child abuse by parents and close relatives. The stakes, nevertheless, are far too high for the order of battle to be ignored, for what is really at stake is the integrity of the most sacred and fundamental institution of American life—the traditional family.

Citizens must examine this issue fairly and objectively and carefully consider its profound ramifications. I am convinced that the issue of child abuse has been and is being used more and more as part of an overall relentless offensive of the ever-growing govern-

ment authority *vis-à-vis* the last check on that authority—
Chesterton's eternal traditional family.

It is no secret that government, in its insatiable thirst for
power, aims at nothing less than the arrogation of the traditional
family's role as the centerpiece of American life. Let me explain.

Under the guise of all-out war against the alleged crime of
child abuse, many observers, as we shall see, believe a cultural war
is being waged by government against the traditional family. Yes,
child abuse, unfortunately, has always occurred, continues to occur
and will likely occur in the future in a small segment of society. The
question therefore is: does it deserve the coverage allotted and the
damage that this coverage inflicts upon the institution of the family?

Many astute observers have come to believe that the crime
of child abuse has been deliberately placed at the forefront of the
social justice debate for ulterior political reasons. They point out that
close examination of the fine print between the published facts and
statistics shows that frequently the figures have been misused and
the problem overstated. One wonders why this is so, and whether
one of the reasons might just be the justification and the perpetua-
tion of government agencies, hosts of social workers, psychologists,
lawyers and welfare bureaucrats—those who partake of the payroll
in the myriad of agencies involved in the investigation of child abuse
cases.

We as physicians, as always, must look at the problem with
truth and objectivity before we become involved and used as
unwitting pawns in what may be a sinister socio-political affair.

The tragedy of all this is that child abuse does exist, that
there are truly dedicated individuals combating this malady and that
truly guilty individuals are not punished commensurate with their
crimes. Frequently, convicted individuals instead of being given jail
terms are used in the bureaucratic game of numbers, figures and
budgets, and given probation and plenty of "therapy" usually at taxpayers' expense.[1]

William Norman Grigg, author of *The Gospel of Revolt:
Feminism Versus Family Values* (Northwest books), asserts that
given today's moral declivity, freedom of sexual expression, and the
modern ethos of immediate gratification (reminiscent of Joseph
Campbell's "follow your bliss" philosophy) where "personal fulfill-

ment for adults," according to Grigg, supersedes the "fulfillment of family responsibilities," we should not be surprised to note an increase in abuse and neglect of children.[2] How else can one explain the well-publicized incident of the couple who went on vacation to Mexico leaving their young children home alone?

The concept of the family has been weakened, not only by the new ethos and new morality but also tangibly by U.S. tax policies. In particular, by tax code provisions that favor couples living together outside of marriage. Yes, cohabitation is favored by tax laws over marriage and this fact is referred to as the "marriage penalty."

Allow me to share with you some specifics. In citing a March 15 issue of *The Washington Times*, Grigg elucidates the fact that if two working people making $12,000 a year each were to get married, given the progressive loss of the standard deductions for families with children over the years and the total marriage penalty—which includes increased taxation and loss of benefits—the loss would add up to more than $3,500; for some low-income families, this loss could mean the necessity "to turn their children over to the state."[1]

But let us return to the issue of child abuse and categorically put some blame where it belongs. Those parents who are genuinely abusive should be held accountable for their criminal acts and prosecuted. If duly convicted, they should serve time and their children placed in carefully investigated foster homes or considered for adoption. Instead, what seems to be happening is that society shares the blame, the guilty parties are not held fully accountable, and the entrenched bureaucracy perpetuates itself.

The flip side of the coin is the plight of those parents falsely accused of child abuse who are made to live through the unspeakable and shocking nightmare of such an accusation. Yes, while there are plenty of accusers in a system that is easily defensible on emotional grounds by the public, nurtured by politicians in the cult of political-expediency and propagated by special interests for their ulterior motives, a mounting number of reputations and lives have been and are being ruined, and an increasing number of families are being torn asunder by bogus accusations. And what is even more devastating is that many of these false allegations have been found to be malicious from the start.[2]

Seth Farber, a psychologist and author of *Madness, Heresy and the Rumor of Angels* (Open Court Press) writes: "Under the guise of providing therapy, social workers and mutual health personnel have prevented criminals from receiving just punishment for their crimes, at the same time, they remove children from good and loving parents."[3]

According to a 1990 Department of Health and Human Services study conducted in 44 states, of 2.7 million reported cases of child abuse or neglect, **75% were not substantiated**.[4] Richard Wexler, author of *Wounded Innocents*, a book that documents the torment and pain of parents falsely accused of child abuse estimates that child abuse allegations range from 58% false charges, 21% neglect (because of poverty) and 8% minor or unspecified physical abuse to 6% sexual abuse and 1% major physical abuse.[5] Guess which figures make the headlines? Just last week my local newspaper's headlines read: "Report Reveals 'Frightening' Child Abuse Figures" and expressed dismay at this crime in which, seemingly, just about every family in America is engaged.[6]

Acts of child abuse, especially severe physical, emotional, or sexual abuse are despicable acts against human nature and society that should be severely punished when it occurs and is proven beyond a reasonable doubt. But, due process must always be given accused parents and they must be considered innocent until proven guilty.

According to Farber, this is how the U.S. Child-Welfare System works today: "The welfare state bureaucracy seeks above all to perpetuate its own existence. It is a monstrous social parasite where the overriding objective—no matter how well intentioned its individual staff member—is to make captive vulnerable individuals, transform them into its clients, foist its 'services' upon them, undermine their autonomy, and ultimately incorporate them into its own parasitic body."[3]

K.L. Billingsley in his article, "Families in Crisis," seems to bolster this dim view of the system. He affirms, "on the flimsiest grounds, social workers can seize children, an action known in the trade as parentectomy. The children are then farmed out to pliable therapists and foster parents." He minces no words in describing the child protection system "as corrupt, incompetent, and motivated by anti-family zealotry."[7]

Douglas Besharov, director of the National Center on Child Abuse between 1975 and 1979 is also critical of the sensational statistics, and he elucidates that of "the more than two million reported incidents of child abuse per year, at least 60% are utterly baseless," and of the remaining 40%, the abuse consists of "emotional or developmental harm that pose no physical danger" to children in 80% of those cases.[8] Moreover, many of the "substantiated" accusations are deliberately directed against home schooling parents—as documented in Missouri by home school advocate Laura Roger—who are anonymously accused of child abuse and threatened by child protection social workers for their home schooling practices, so as to coerce them back into the system.[8]

And there is more, Lowry and Samuelson explain that even after the fight to take the children away from their parents is "won" by the government's social workers, the lot of the children is not likely to improve in the hands of the state. They cite a study in Baltimore by the head of the Department of Research at New York University School of Social Work that "found that 28% of the children in foster care had been abused while in the system."[4] Even the liberal ACLU Children's Project admits "that a child in the care of the state is ten times more likely to be abused than one in the care of his parents."[4] The message is clear then, unless culpability is proven beyond a reasonable doubt, children are better off in their own homes with their biological or adoptive parents within the fabric of the traditional family.

In the article, "The Politics of Child Abuse," Grigg documents a catalogue of cases of falsely-accused parents and the resultant denial of justice: family bankruptcies filed by parents burdened with legal debts and foster care bills incurred in their own defense, a defense mounted by parents against a state which has unlimited wealth (shouldered by taxpayers) and power to prosecute with impunity.[2] It goes without saying that cases in which parents are falsely accused or there is a shadow of a doubt—publicity and usurpation of the presumption of being considered innocent until proven guilty, trampling upon due-process rights, psychological torment undergone by parents served with these malicious accusations, not to mention the irreparable disruption and destruction of families—represents a diabolical travesty of justice.

The "Child Protection" program suspects all parents who are brought to their attention by zealous social workers. Dr. Dean Edell, a syndicated radio talk-show host physician, recently aired studies that show how easily young children are persuaded to "create evidence" by mere suggestions and leading questions by authority figures, such as social workers, psychologists, and by extension, any child protection agency worker. The recent discovery of the *False Memory Syndrome* whereby therapists treating susceptible individuals, who have sought treatment for depression or some other psychological problems, have been impregnated with false recollections is most frightening. Yes, adults seeking counselling for sundry psychological disorders have been and are being inculcated or implanted with perverse ideas or false memories that their present problems (or their own life shortcomings) stem from their having been abused or molested as children by one of their parents or close relatives—all through the coaching of determined and overzealous social workers or psychologists.[1,2]

To counteract the growing trend of such "tardy discovery of child abuse," groups of genuinely-concerned child protection workers, psychologists, and accused parents have founded support groups such as The False Memory Foundation. With their newsletters and education programs, they hope to counteract the "disreputable therapeutic practices and ideological prejudices" of the Child Abuse Survivor Movement—but the members of these support groups have their hands full. The NOW Legal Defense Fund has put together a Legal Resource Kit—catering to adults who have "suddenly discovered" that they were abused as children, and are referred to as "survivors." Those who are interested are invited to file "survivor" lawsuits. One (usually the father) or both of their now aging parents are then sued for damages. Grigg calls attention to the fact that under the provisions enumerated by child abuse activists, such as feminists Ellen Bass and Laura Davis in their book, *The Courage to Heal*: "...If you are unable to remember any specific instances of abuse like the ones mentioned above but still have a feeling that something happened to you, it probably did...if you think you were abused and your life shows the symptoms, then you were."[9]

Not surprisingly, these authors who are not psychologists

urge lawsuits as a vehicle for "raising society's consciousness about adult recovery" from childhood abuse.

There is no question that the child abuse theme, as a front of the cultural war being waged in America, is an explosive issue which, if lost, not only would undermine the right to privacy for individuals falsely accused, but would result in the net loss of due-process, equal protection under the law, and other constitutional safeguards, such as the basic American legal premise of being considered innocent until proven guilty. Meanwhile, attorney-litigators have drilled into another money-making oil well of opportunity, while prosecutors gain fame and a step up the ladder of political aspiration.

Uncontested and unchallenged this issue could tear asunder the fundamental and sacred concept of the traditional family. Do we want to break down and eliminate the traditional family and give our children to the state as in ancient Sparta?

According to the Greek historian and biographer Plutarch (A.D. 46—c.A.D. 120), in the ancient Greek city-state of Sparta, King Lycurgus (fl. 9th Century B.C.) abolished the family, and the children were made the property of the militaristic Spartan state. The statist collectivist system of Sparta was set up to rear strong-bodied obedient soldiers; the unfortunate weaklings were eliminated without reservation. Families lost their children and society was totally subordinate and subservient to government, a totalitarian militaristic state.[10]

As we physicians know well, the family structure is an integral component of society, necessary for the psychological and physical nurturing and healing of patients. Family support is basic to healing and essential to health: Let us fortify not destroy it.

Physicians must look at both sides of the dilemma, examine the data and make objective assessments before jumping onto another bandwagon of political expediency. Even with the reality of the existence of genuine child abuse cases, it becomes self-evident that the rearing of children by parents within the concept of the traditional family strengthens society and must be preserved, and should not be allowed to be supplanted by another dangerous, unenumerated power of the state.

**REFERENCES**

1. Grigg WN. The war against the family. The New American 1993; 9 (10):73-74.

2. Grigg WN. The politics of child abuse. The New American 1992; 8 (18):23-30.

3. Farber S. The real abuse. National Review 1993; 45 (7):44-50.

4. Lowry R, Samuelson R. How many battered children? National Review 1993; 45 (7):46.

5. Wexler R. Wounded innocents. Cited by Lowry R, and Samuelson R, op. cit., p. 46.

6. The Associated Press, The Macon Telegraph, August 4, 1993.

7. Billingsley KL. Families in crisis. Reason 1992, cited by Grigg WN, The politics of child abuse, op. cit., p. 25.

8. Besharov D. Cited by Grigg WN, The war against the family, op. cit., pp. 73-74.

9. Bass E, Davis E. The courage to heal. Cited by Grigg WN, The politics of child abuse, op. cit., p. 26.

10. Plutarch's Lives. The Dryden Translation; Random House, The Modern Library, New York, 1984; pp. 49-74.

(OCTOBER, 1993)


*[In May of 1994, jurors sent a clear message when they found that two therapists conjured up false memories of child abuse in a patient whose "recovered memory" alleged her father had raped her as a child.*

*The jury awarded $500,000 to Mr. Gary Ramona, aged 50, whose life was wrecked by his daughter's allegations. As a result of the accusations, Mr. Ramona was divorced by his wife and lost his $400,000-a-year marketing job as a winery executive.*

*Mr. Ramona's attorney, Richard Harrington, was quoted by the Associated Press (May 15, 1994) as calling the trial "a warning to psychotherapists who carelessly use the concept of recovered memories." The verdict was expected to have and is having a profound effect in tempering unsubstantiated accusations of child abuse by "recovered memories," by sending the signal that the use of repressed memories (false memory syndrome) to destroy the family unit will result in legal repercussions.]*

CHAPTER 7

# *THE TRUE NUMBERS OF UNINSURED AMERICANS*

*A half-truth is a whole lie.*
Jewish Proverb

*Anything repeated three times in Washington becomes fact.*
Eugene McCarthy

In a previous article,[1] I wrote that, "Only 4% of the [American] population lacks health insurance for two years or longer," and hinted at the fact the actual number of truly chronically uninsured and underinsured was less than the number the media and the Congressional Budget Office (CBO) had promulgated before and during the Presidential campaign—the 34-37 million so often quoted. Well, it turns out Dr. Francis Davis, publisher of *Private Practice*, has also disclosed in a recent editorial the work of Alan Reynolds, director of economic research at the Hudson Institute in Indianapolis, who called the much touted number of uninsured "this year's (1992) big lie" in a *Detroit News* article.[2]

The CBO has done it again. As you will remember, it was the CBO which both suggested and estimated that millions of dollars in revenues could be obtained by "soaking the rich" in the form of taxation of luxury yachts. What really happened was that "the rich" stopped buying the luxury boats. With orders down, revenues fell and hundreds of workers lost their jobs.

Moreover, the CBO was one of the government agencies that was responsible for the campaign rhetoric that propounded the erroneous notion that billions of dollars could be saved if we were to proceed with national health insurance. Their fiscal report contradicted other studies conducted on the subject, including the Pepper Commission, as well as those figures compiled by various privately-funded think tanks, such as the Washington-based Heritage Foundation and the Dallas-based National Center for Policy Analysis, which have predicted additional expenses in the order of $250-$350 billion in health care expenditures annually if national health insurance is implemented in the U.S.[3] Fortunately, with the horror stories coming out of Canada, national health insurance, per se, has been put temporarily on the backburner.

But let us now return to the issue of the actual number of uninsured in America. Reynolds reveals the CBO looked at a 1-month "snapshot" to come up with the high figures. This misleading figure does not represent the needy who are truly uninsured because they cannot afford health care insurance. As I stated in my article, "60% of them are actually working adults and their families; many of them are self-employed or starting their own businesses."[1] Reynolds explains that this number also represents many people who are changing jobs or young people going on to school or who choose not to buy insurance because at that point in their lives, their education or buying their first home, for example, were more important to them than obtaining health insurance. Those numbers should not be added implicitly when discussing the genuinely chronically uninsured or those unfortunate individuals who *cannot* obtain insurance because of pre-existing conditions or chronic illness.

The Census Bureau, more appropriately, "instead of taking a snapshot of a single month, took a moving picture over 28 months during the late 1980s and found that 4% of all persons lacked coverage for the entire period." What this meant was that fewer than 10 million Americans lack health insurance coverage for a protracted period of time. This information is more in tune with figures published as far back as January 1991 by the *Physician Financial News* which reported on an Urban Institute study showing that "for half the uninsured, the uninsured spells end within 4 months, and [of the number of uninsured] only 15% are uninsured for longer than 2 years."[4]

Thus, it appears that 5 to 10 million people would represent the truly chronically uninsured (or uninsurable) and the actual figure that would need government-provided *vouchers* if we were to proceed with the **patient-oriented, free-market** approach to medical care that I described in my article. The rest of us (the other 96% of the population) would, or rather should, then buy our own health insurance. Health insurance should then be 100% deductible for the individual buying it and taxable only for workers getting it as benefits from their employers.

Implementation of the *Medisave* (also known as Medical Savings Accounts or Individual Medical Accounts) concept of health care delivery would provide universal access to the best health care available in the world. Moreover, it would give the individual incentive not only to obtain medical insurance but also to seek high-deductible, catastrophic insurance coverage. The *Medisave* would be used for small medical bills and out-of-pocket expenses. The system, therefore, does provide incentive for individual fiscal responsibility and promotes high quality health care for all Americans. It would preserve the patient-doctor relationship, the patient's choice of physicians, and autonomy on the part of both the patient and the doctor—all aspects of the plan conceived within the private sector.

More than 100 Congressmen, including the majority of Republicans and many Democrats, support the establishment of the *Medisave* concept (including vouchers, tax-refundable credits for high-deductible insurance, and tax-free medical IRAs) as the centerpiece of health care delivery for the future. And since none of the other health care schemes, though highly publicized by the mainstream media and health care "experts," have a majority of votes in either the House or Senate, there is still a significant chance that the **patient-oriented, free-market** health care option could be enacted by Congress.

Moreover, Terree P. Wasley writing in *Private Practice* reports that, "currently only 17 out of the 75-plus members of the Conservative Democratic Forum (CDF) support the managed-competition approach."[5]

The final battle may be hard fought but we must remember the words of George Elliot (1819-1880), the English novelist who wrote, "Any coward can fight a battle when he is sure of winning." Given the fact that highly debatable public initiatives, especially those concerning health care, are said to be lost in Congress by razor-thin margins (typically less than 40 votes), there is still considerable room for victory by the physicians and their patients. But success may only be possible if enough physicians mobilize to fight in what seems at this point the most crucial battle of all—the battle for the preservation of high-quality medical care without rationing and within the purview of the individual-based, patient-doctor relationship, Hippocratic ethics, and its implementation via the private sector.

Let us not ask for less than the best for our patients. As Thomas Percival wrote in his *Medical Ethics* (1803):

*The physicians and surgeons should not suffer themselves to be restrained by parsimonious considerations, from prescribing wine, and drugs even of high price, when required in diseases of extraordinary malignity and danger. The efficacy of every medicine is proportionate to its purity and goodness....But when drugs of inferior quality are employed, it is requisite to administer them in larger doses, and to continue to use them a longer period of time; circumstances which, probably, more than counterbalance any savings in their original price.*[6]

The battle is not over yet. There is hope. Be informed and vigilant and become involved in the health care debate, and join our mission to rescue medicine from the clutches of government.

### REFERENCES

1. Faria MA Jr. Crisis in health care delivery—rescuing medicine from the clutches of government. J Med Assoc Ga 1992;81(11):615-620. See Chapter 4.

2. Davis FA. So much for this year's big lie. Private Practice 1992;24(11):20.

3. Goodman JC. An Agenda for Solving America's Health Care Crisis, 1991. National Center for Policy Analysis, 12655 North Central Expressway, Suite 720, Dallas, Tx. 75243. (214) 386-6276.

4. Physicians Financial News, January 15, 1991. Reported in AAPS News 1991;47(3):2.

5. Wasley TP. Clintons consider health care options. Private Practice 1993;25(3):11.

6. Percival T. Medical Ethics. Chauncey D. Leake (Ed.), Williams and Wilkins Co., Baltimore, Maryland, 1927, pp. 74-75.

(MAY, 1993)

## CHAPTER 8

# THE VICISSITUDES OF HEALTH CARE REFORM

*The man who produces while others dispose of his product is a slave.*
Ayn Rand (1905-1982)

*The man who makes no mistakes does not usually make anything.*
Edward John Phelps (1822-1900)

*They [The Makers of the Constitution] conferred, as against the government, the right to be left alone—the most comprehensive of rights and the right most valued by civilized man.*
Louis D. Brandeis (1928)

*Patriotism means to stand by the country. It does not mean to stand by the President or any other public official save exactly to the degree in which he himself stands by the country. It is patriotic to support him insofar as he efficiently serves the country. It is unpatriotic not to oppose him to the extent that by inefficiency or otherwise he fails in his duty to stand by the country.*
Theodore Roosevelt (1858-1919)

Have you heard the tale told by Rep. Fortney "Pete" Stark (D-CA), at the AMA summit meeting in Washington, DC, earlier this year (1993).[1] Congressman Stark "had just been given a glowing, almost syrupy introduction" by Dr. James Todd of the AMA, and then told the following tale, *Death by Varuba:*

*"I'll illustrate the problem you [AMA physicians] face with a story. A Dr. Sammons and a Dr. Todd were off the coast of some unnamed continent where people still practiced cannibalism and other rituals. Their ship crashed and they were lost in the jungle.*

*The leader, Chief Stark, found these infidels invading his sacred turf and brought them to the compound.*

*The Chief said, "Gentlemen, you have invaded our secret space and you have two choices. You may chose either death or Varuba."*

*Well, Sammons just came apart: "I have a family to go*

*back to, I'm just finishing my term, I'm waiting to hand over the reigns of this organization to Dr. Todd, and I can't die. I just can't. I will take Varuba."*

*And Chief Stark said, "Very well, let Varuba begin."*

*Jim Todd had to sit and watch the most inhumane torture, evisceration, pulling out of fingernails, sodomizing—the worst kind of treatment that anybody except Chief Stark could imagine. As this went on, Chief Stark turned to Dr. Todd and said, "Now your choice."*

*Jim said, "I'm not a strong man. I'll take death."*

*Whereupon the Chief said, "Very well, death by Varuba!"*

"This is somewhat the position that you are all in [with] healthcare reform today," Pete Stark arrogantly, boldly, and scornfully told the assembled AMA physicians.[1]

This derision and ridicule of the medical profession by such a health authority figure as Rep. Stark went unreported by the mainstream media and organized medical publications, except for the *AAPS News Bulletin.* The incident is especially troubling, since the AMA has gone out of its way to placate Congressman Stark at every opportunity. Nevertheless, Stark has repeatedly opposed organized medicine in every health care policy decision; this, despite the fact that he ranked number one among members of Congress in the receipt of political contributions, collecting $497,250 for the decade ending June 30, 1991.

Common Cause reported that of that large sum, Stark amassed a whopping $203,200 from medical political action committees (PACs), thereby positioning himself as the number two recipient of funds from the ranks of organized medicine.[2]

Congressman Stark's speech and actions not only reveal his contempt for the leadership of the AMA but also that not all members of Congress can be influenced or cajoled with PAC money. I must admit that, to his credit, despite the huge sums of money he has received from medical PACs, he has remained committed to his liberal ideology and principles, including his single-payer national health care plan modeled after Medicare. His vision remains the expansion of the Medicare system from its present 35 million elderly Americans to the incorporation of all 250 million American citizens. Medicare cost control mechanisms including DRGs, RBRVS, Volume Performance Standards, and intimidation tactics would all be part of the program, if he could get his way.

In fact, now that the long-awaited Clinton health care reform plan is out, after much grooming and many revisions, none of us should be too surprised to find many of Stark's ideas webbed into the plan. For example, a Standard Benefit Package incorporating long-term care, home health care, and prescription drugs, all of which Stark wanted, are part of the package.

Now that Clinton's health care package has been officially unveiled,* it will only be a matter of time before my prediction of last February materializes, namely that, "President Clinton's Health Care reform package will have a veneer of capitalism covering a hard core of socialism...."[3]

Yes, the plan has an employer-mandated as well as a public-financing mechanism, borrowing from the "Play or Pay" scheme of yore that was espoused by candidate Bill Clinton during his presidential campaign. In addition, the plan calls for universal coverage to be phased in and provided through multiple tiers of bureaucracy, the most conspicuous of which would be the Health Insurance Purchasing Cooperatives (HIPCs). The plan follows the outline of the AAPS report that described another tier of administrative bureaucracy, the State Health Boards, appointed by the governors.[4] These State Health Boards will define the Standard Benefits Package, and through the third tier, the Regional Health Alliances, will make sure that premiums are collected. The Regional Health Alliances will project a semblance of (managed) competition, would make sure that the per capita-based budget operates within its limits, and that all enrollees are accepted "regardless of medical condition" (or health habits). Fee-for-service medicine will be allowed to operate, at least in paper, but is expected to be phased out as the plan gets under way.[4]

Despite the opposition of organized medicine to price fixing, the Administration will set limits on health care spending either by congressional action or as mandated by the National Health Board, a fourth tier of bureaucracy. This, despite the fact that this detail was not part of the managed competition scheme at its inception, and that prior to his inauguration, Clinton was character-

*The Health Security Act of 1993.

istically vague about global budgets, saying only, "the devil's in the details."

The President's plan is under fire not only from the Right, but also from the Left. Already the Congressional Budget Office (CBO)—the same "nonpartisan" office that erroneously created the inflated "37 million" of chronically uninsured and predicted that millions of dollars in revenues could be collected by "soaking the rich" via taxation of the luxury yacht industry[5]—is posing a problem for the Administration. The CBO insists that managed competition would not save any money, would still leave 25 million people uninsured, and would augment health care spending by $19 billion. According to the CBO, a single-payer government-provided system (presumably à la Stark or concocted Canadian style) "would cover everybody and would save $150 billion."[4]

My fellow physicians, think again if you feel that we can lower our guard. The single-payer government-run system is not dead. Like the news about Mark Twain, its death "has been greatly exaggerated."

We should continue to fight for patient-oriented free-market medicine with tax-free medical saving accounts, individual responsibility, and the preservation of the patient-doctor relationship. For if we are not victorious, when all is said and done and the oxymoronic managed competition option is deemed a failure—buried under its own bureaucratic weight—the only option left in the brave New World Order will be socialized medicine, rationing, and even outright denial of care.

Physicians can no longer afford to be meek, humble, and acquiescent, staying on the sidelines in the midst of the tempestuous battle raging in our communities. We must rally behind medical savings accounts (MSAs) coupled with high-deductible, catastrophic insurance coverage, Hippocratic medicine, and freedom of choice with patient autonomy.

It has been said that the states, as far as health care reform, will be the laboratories of democracy, but those states which choose to use this refrain to rush ahead to the abattoir of managed competition such as Minnesota and Florida, or which plan to put cost containment above quality, rationing health care under the aegis of the state, such as Oregon, and "preemptively surrender"[6] will have long term the most to lose.

Besides, borrowing from the Greek sage Solon (c. 639—c. 559 B.C.), even Congressman Stark has come up with a substantive and meaningful idea, which, although likely to make hairs stand on end among his fellow members of Congress, should be welcome by the citizenry. Stark has declared that "the public is demanding that Congress include itself under all laws that it passes for others. After all, what is good for the goose is good for the gander."[7] What most people do not know is that Congress and federal employees are covered by an excellent health care plan—deeply imbued in free choice and free-market concepts, and one from which the Heritage Foundation proposals borrow heavily.[8]

So, my dear conferees do not despair in this hour of uncertainty. All is not lost. Indeed, the battle has just begun. Physicians have a professional obligation, a sacred duty, to be politically active. We can no longer afford to be silent and passive; otherwise, we will be run over by the machinery of the bureaucratic and increasingly autocratic state. Or, are we to believe along the lines of Georges Clemenceau who said, "War is too important to be left to the generals," that health care is too important to be left to the physicians? And if we do not take the initiative, then who will? The bureaucrats?

### REFERENCES

1. Griffin GC. Death By Varuba! Congressman arrogantly tells doctor. Post Grad Med 1993;93(7):13-16.
2. Faria MA, Jr. On managed competition and other catch 22 items. J. Med. Assoc. Ga. 1993;82(6):269-271. See Chapter 20.
3. Faria MA Jr. The medical gulag. J. Med. Assoc. Ga. 1993;82(2):56.2. See Chapter 23.
4. AAPS News, Legislative Supplement. Association of American Physicians and Surgeons 1993;49(9):S1-S2.
5. Faria MA Jr. On the true number of uninsured Americans. J. Med. Assoc. Ga. 1993;82(5)203-204. See Chapter 7.
6. Price TE. Fear, anxiety, and resistance: those old familiar hallmarks of change. J. Med. Assoc. Ga. 1993;82(8):420-423.
7. The Macon Telegraph, September 23, 1993; Quoting Congressman "Pete" Stark (D-CA).
8. Moffit R. Solving the health care crisis: a prescription for reform. J. Med. Assoc. Ga. 1993;82(6):293-296.

(NOVEMBER, 1993)

CHAPTER 9

# THE DATA BANK IN BIG BROTHER'S SCHEME OF THINGS

*Unless the people, through unified action, arise and take charge of their Government, they will find that their Government has taken charge of them. Independence and liberty will be gone and the general public will find itself in a condition of servitude to an aggregation of organized and selfish ambitions.*

Calvin Coolidge (30th President of the U.S. [1923-1929])
and Alfred E. Smith (Joint Statement issued October 12, 1932)

*Government is not reason, it is not eloquence—it is force. Like fire, it is a dangerous servant and a fearful master; never, for a moment, should it be left to irresponsible action.*

George Washington (1732-1799)

### A MEDICAL ABERRATION

I began to wage war against the National Practitioners Data Bank (the "Data Bank" or NPDB) as soon as the mechanics, meaning, and implications of its existence became clear. I wrote a scathing editorial* outlining my objections, predictions, and suggestions.[1] Now, as events have unfolded, I am sorry to note the predictions have proven to be inauspiciously correct and many of the suggestions unhappily have not been (and are not being) heeded. What is more, it is becoming crystal clear that big government—Big Brother—does not intend to sever this abominable entity, but plans to expand the Data Bank's role in their own war against medical practitioners, using it as an instrument of fear and intimidation.

There is no evidence whatsoever that the Data Bank has fulfilled (or contributed significantly to) any of its originally stated missions: To encourage peer review; impede unscrupulous, unethical, or incompetent physicians from moving from states (where they have been disciplined) to others where their disciplining

*The contents of this editorial, materialized as a strongly worded resolution, aroused considerable discussion at the MAG House of Delegates in the 1991 and 1992 sessions. The final resolved read as follows: "RESOLVED, that MAG take immediate action through legislative avenues to seek the repeal of The Data Bank, as violative of the civil liberties of American physicians."

actions are not known and where they may establish new medical practices unhindered; or to enhance the overall quality of health care delivery. Yet, confidential data on physicians continues to accumulate within the authoritarian confines of the Data Bank; while Big Brother's surveillance and information-gathering capabilities have grown exponentially and ominously via the activities of this entity.

From the time the Data Bank became operational on September 1, 1990 to February of 1991, it had filed approximately 12,000 pieces of information concomitant with over 300,000 requests (or queries) for information.[2] By August 31, 1991 (the first year of operation), the intrusive repository had jumped up to a whopping 781,247 requests (averaging 3000 queries/day) and had collected 18,561 adverse action and malpractice payouts which were irrevocably and permanently filed. A total of 85% of the entries, in fact, were malpractice payments. By April 30, 1993, a new record had been reached with 2,233,061 queries.[3] Today, the entity contains information on approximately 13,000 physicians and other health practitioners "who have been sued for malpractice or disciplined by a state medical licensing board."[4] Yet, Big Brother has failed to demonstrate to anyone's satisfaction that the Data Bank has succeeded in any of its purported objectives.

I continue to believe that this abominable entity should be dismantled for a variety of reasons. I will elaborate on my previous objections as follows:

• *The Data Bank is discriminatory* because no other profession is subjected (or deliberately singled out) to such mandated blacklisting. The medical profession remains the most scrutinized and regulated profession in America.[5-9] Nevertheless, I now believe, after witnessing the further growth of the regulatory bureaucracy and the police powers of the state, that in due time, other professions and trades will inevitably follow down this same authoritarian path.

Even within the medical profession itself, the Data Bank is discriminatory because some specialties such as Orthopedics, General Surgery, Obstetrics, and Neurosurgery are disproportionately affected because of the high-risk nature of those specialties.

• *The Data Bank violates the civil rights of physicians*

because practitioners have little or no recourse to redress their grievances. A recent report proclaims that "physicians have been given the chance to get their side of the story permanently on record without filing a formal dispute."[9] The naked reality is that not only have physicians been denied the presumption of being innocent until proven guilty, before being permanently filed (and defiled) in the Data Bank, but strict limits have been placed on their purported defense. The written defense "can be no more than 600 characters, including punctuation and spacing—or about 85 to 100 words."[9]

• *The Data Bank violates due process and the equal protection of the law* clauses of the Fifth and Fourteenth Amendments to the Constitution that should protect American physicians as U.S. citizens. The Data Bank cannot guarantee (even with electronic storing, retrieval, and responding to queries) that the information obtained will be used for its intended purpose or that such information will remain confidential. All 50 states have freedom of information acts which makes access to these files a possibility. Erroneous release of information resulting in deleterious effects upon the professional life of a physician is no longer an unlikely or remote possibility; it has already happened.[10]

Moreover, disputed or inaccurate information can result in a permanent blot on the physician's reputation in an otherwise unblemished and caring career. Simply stated, the Data Bank remains a government-mandated instrument of intimidation with the resultant oppressive national blacklisting of physicians.

• *The Data Bank has neither improved the quality of health care delivery and the patient-doctor relationship*, nor has it improved the image of physicians in the eyes of the public. Now more than ever, physicians are reluctant to participate in peer review, not only because of antitrust provisions unrelated to the Data Bank, but also because they are aware that their quality assurance activities may result in the irretrievable loss of a colleague's reputation...and permanent filing in the Data Bank. In fact, peer review activities decreased by 10% immediately following its inception in 1990, amidst the understandable fear of the Data Bank provisions and anticipated consequences of its implementation.[11]

Like defensive medicine, the Data Bank has contributed to the siege mentality and adversarial climate in which physicians practice today, supplying additional evidence that indeed we are under attack by third-party payers, Medicare-sanctioning bureaucrats, self-styled medical ethicists, and particularly, attorney-litigators and government health care policymakers—the latter already bent on taking over medical care.

• *The Data Bank is inherently unfair* for at least two reasons. One, maloccurrences prior to its implementation were included in the files. Two, some physicians were more equal than others and were exempted, such as those in the VA hospital system and the Department of Defense, which conveniently chose not to participate.[12]

• *The Data Bank is an unnecessary waste of resources.* Besides adding to health care costs per se, it fans the fire of defensive medicine, one of the greatest contributors to escalating health care costs. Moreover, I have been told by hospital administrators that they do not get the information they need, and often, the information they do get is irrelevant.[1,8,11] Yet, plaintiffs' attorneys can query the Data Bank if they can prove that hospitals are not complying with this act (that is, mandated querying for new or renewing applicants). What is even more embarrassing for the Data Bank proponents is that state licensing boards, recognizing the inadequacies and superfluity of data, and the additional costs incurred through its use, have shown little interest in the Data Bank's repository. In the first two years, less than half of the boards "had requested information, accounting for less than 0.1% of all queries."[7] Yet, these were the disciplining agencies that supposedly most needed the data!

### HISTORICALLY—A TIMID COUNTER-ATTACK

In 1991 and 1992, experts predicted that the Data Bank would collapse under its own weight. Some of us were not so sure, and we pushed (apparently not hard enough) to shove it over the precipice of extinction.[13] Unfortunately, the push at the national level (AMA) was not of the same vigorous intensity as that of ours at the state level, and today, the abominable entity is alive and well—and thriving.

While the delegates to the AMA House of Delegates were pressing for abolition, the Board of Trustees of the AMA opted "to pursue vigorous remedial action to correct all operational problems with the NPDB."[14] Moreover, it recommended that "small claim payments, less than $30,000, no longer be reported to the NPDB."[14] These insufficient proposals, needless to say, were too timid and too vacuous to force the odious entity down the precipitous cliff. Suffice to say, the AMA leadership was playing softball when government bureaucrats were playing hardball.

And yes, self-styled consumer advocates and their allies are likewise playing hardball on this uneven playing field. For instance, Dr. Sidney Wolfe of the Public Citizen Health Research Group (an organization founded by attorney Ralph Nader) has long advocated a fully open Data Bank with unrestricted access for the public.[9] Answering the call, Congressman Ron Wyden (D-OR) introduced a bill to open the NPDB to the public, "all adverse actions would be reported to the public through free, semiannual booklets distributed to public libraries."[7] In tandem with the Health Security Act of 1993, which calls for opening the Data Bank for "repeat offenders," the Wyden proposal would disclose practitioners with "two or more incidents"—a sort of "two strikes and you are out" proposition tailored for physicians.*

In 1991, regarding the Public Citizen Health Research Group, I wrote: *"Among other things, this group is also advocating consumer access to the Data Bank purportedly to determine 'how often a doctor is sued for malpractice.' This is absurd. They want access to all privileged information on file. Unless we physicians stand up and fight for our rights, we will see the usurpation of whatever remains of our constitutional due process."*[1]

Moreover, under Congressman Wyden's proposal, the state licensing boards would be required to query the Data Bank before granting or renewing licenses, and even report license denials. "Board officials [State Medical Boards] claim the federal repository duplicates their own data collection and, at $10 a shot, regular queries would be too costly for the underfunded boards."[7]

---

* The bill authorizes public access to all adverse actions and to malpractice payment reports for practitioners with two or more incidents; and requires medical boards to report license denials, not just revocations and suspensions. All adverse actions would be reported to the public through free booklets distributed semi-annually to public libraries.

Needless to say, with the incarnation of the Data Bank we have in place an unconstitutional entity demanding regulatory overkill for physicians; we have in place an authoritarian bureaucracy creating more red tape while ominously usurping individual liberties, and needlessly squandering money at taxpayers' expense.

To the partial credit of the AMA, the latest proposal to open records in the Data Bank to the public has finally drawn criticism from the organization. AMA trustee, Thomas R. Reardon M.D., has pointed out, "even when a doctor is innocent of any wrongdoing, malpractice settlements occur in order to save the greater expense of a trial....These settlements are reported to the Data Bank as if the physicians had done something wrong."[7] The AMA opposes releasing malpractice information through the Data Bank. But this stance, obviously, will not be of itself enough to effect what is truly appropriate: outright, immediate abolition.

As things now stand, the Data Bank threatens to remain another instrument of intimidation fitting nicely in Big Brother's scheme of things: the much touted provider waste, fraud, and abuse that needs to be stamped out to solve the "crisis." Physicians need to oppose the NPDB, not only on practical and economic grounds but also *on principle*; and to work more vigorously to effect the fall, to shove this aberration once and for all down the precipice of extinction.

### REFERENCES

1. Faria MA Jr. The data bank—why it should be abolished. J Med Assoc Ga 1991;(9):477-478.
2. Morgan N. Medical staff meeting. HCA Coliseum Medical Centers, February 12, 1991.
3. Oberman L. Data bank access debate. Am Med News 1993;May 24/31.
4. Data bank bill introduced. American College of Surgeons Bulletin 1994;(6):5.
5. Page L. Doctors discipline total: depends on who's counting. Am Med News 1991;Feb 18:37-38.
6. Gianelli DM. Book reports disciplinary actions against physicians. Am Med News 1991;Feb 21.
7. Oberman L. Bill would unlock data bank. Am Med News 1994;May 9:1,10.
8. Faria MA Jr. Vandals at the Gates of Medicine—Historic Perspectives on the Battle Over Health Care Reform. Hacienda Publishing, Inc.,Macon, Georgia, in press.
9. Practitioner bank adds defense option. Medical Tribune for the Family Practitioner. April 21, 1994.
10. Sullivan R. Letter to the editor. Am Med News 1991;March 25:15.

11. Page L. Which malpractice payouts need to be reported. Am Med News 1991;Dec 16:9.

12. Jaffe BM. Big brother is looking askance at you. Surg Rounds 1991;(3):183-185.

13. Resolutions on the National Practitioner's Data Bank passed by the House of Delegates of MAG 1991, 1992, and 1993.

14. AMA Policy Compendium. Board of Trustees report (A-92). Policy 355.990, 355.999, 355.993.

(SEPTEMBER, 1994)

Chapter 10

# AT THE BRINK OF THE ABYSS

*Was Ayn Rand correct when she wrote that the difference between a welfare state and a totalitarian state is only a matter of time?*

*There are frighteningly accurate predictions of the present government and corporate rape of Medicine in Ayn Rand's* Atlas Shrugged. *In the novel, the government decides to control new, lightweight, and exceedingly strong metal—symbolic of the metal of one's mind, one's soul—one's productivity—and enacts laws making ownership of Rearden Metal a virtual right. Hank Rearden's response is noteworthy: "'A sale...requires the seller's consent....There's Rearden Metal. Drive down there with your trucks—like any other looter....I won't shoot you, as you know I can't—take as much ...as you wish....Don't try to send me payment. I won't accept.'"[1]*

*Rearden made it impossible for the government to pretend that the seizure was a morally righteous transaction. When the government's policy resulted in internal strife and decay, increasingly drastic measures were implemented, resulting in tight central control of the economy under the dictates of a Unification Board. Wage and price controls were a central feature. Freedom was ruthlessly suppressed, in the name of security, stability, and full equality.*

*I wish that I could read Ayn Rand's words and dismiss them as sheer paranoid invention—but they were truly prophetic. It is clear that the federal government has already injected policies into the Medicare program which are all too evocative of the image of the totalitarian state painted in* Atlas Shrugged. *Our government is converting Rand's nightmarish scenario into deadly serious reality.*

*Radical changes are in store for American Medicine, which our government is manipulating in a manner all too redolent of the actions taken by Rand's fictitious Unification Board.*

Joseph Scherzer, M.D.
From *"The Holocaust Memorial, Ayn Rand, and Politics in Pre-Revolutionary New York: Lessons for Today."*

The most important issue that physicians are facing today and will be confronting during this entire decade, whether or not the Health Security Act of 1993 passes completely or in part, will remain the dilemma of preserving the practice of private medicine in the face of a public clamoring for change incited by the media and politicians, coupled with an ever-expanding omnipresent government whose bureaucratic tentacles extend everywhere, seemingly destined to control, not only American medicine, but all aspects of American life. The gargantuan task confronting practicing physicians is whether they have the courage to educate their patients to the grim reality of what is transpiring under the guise of "reform"—before we all stumble into the abyss of socialized (corporate or single-payer) medicine and total government control.

This task is also daunting because the American public appears to have been seduced by the sweet-sounding melodies of "free care" sung by the politician-sirens who, notwithstanding the fact that we are swimming in an ocean of red ink (the national debt approaches $4.5 trillion), promise an empyrean paradise and deliver earthly misery (despite spending $3.6 trillion on welfare programs since the inception of the Great Society).[2]

Moreover, seduced by the treacherous illusion of government as provider—of "cradle-to-grave" free care and services—the public has come to believe that moral conduct and behavior are relative and that there are no absolute rights or wrongs (*moral relativism*), only the hedonistic reality of immediate gratification (*situational ethics*). We should not be surprised then to learn that 80% of diseases can be linked to unhealthy lifestyles or even self-destructive behaviors, yet we expect doctors and medicine to keep us young and healthy to a ripe old age![3] And now, on top of this, the Clinton administration promises a Health Security Card* and "health care that can not be taken away," and an ethereal right to free government-provided health care.

What the public really is going to get is the loss of freedom to choose their physician, place of treatment, and choice of treatment plan; rationing will become inevitable; quality will be sacrificed under the guise of cost-effectiveness; and the citizenry, additionally, would be placed in mortal danger of losing their liberties, for like in Nazi Germany, the Health Security Card would be used (and is already intended to be) as an identification card where the most

* In fact, Ron Paul, M.D. writing in the December 1993 issue of *The Free Market* cautions, "the card's computer chip could contain 60 pages of data per person, to be updated at will...[containing] your entire federal dossier, including tax, employment, medical, marital, child, passport, and other records....For the government, knowledge is power, and the more it knows about us...the easier it is to control us." Dr. Paul is now a U.S. Congressman from Texas.

intimate of information, personal health, and even the health care costs incurred by the person in question (to the state) and other particulars will be stored in a national data file monitored by Big Brother. We are moving Left towards socialism, collectivism, and bureaucracy.

What a shame! This at a time when others have found that communism (translate: socialism) doesn't work. Communism has fallen, and Central and Eastern Europe are looking at truly free market economies. They do not want the socialist or Keynesian economists that we have sent to advise them during their transition. They want free-market economists from the Chicago or Austrian school of economics. Boris Yeltsin has renounced socialism, wants Russia to have a free-market economy, and yearns for his country to join the West and NATO! This is what President Boris Yeltsin said in a speech in Moscow on June 1, 1991: "Our country has not been lucky....It was decided to carry out this Marxist experiment on us...It has simply pushed us off the path the world's civilized countries have taken....In the end we proved that there is no place for this idea."[4] Even Sweden, the darling of the soft Left, has begun to roll back socialism. Cradle-to-grave socialism in Sweden and the rest of Scandinavia is collapsing under its own bloated bureaucratic weight. While those countries which have experienced socialism themselves are looking now toward the Right, as painful as the transition has been and continues to be, we move relentlessly toward the Left.

It is inexplicable that so many of our own political leaders look for further government intrusion and bureaucracy to remedy the problems of American society.[5] If you doubt that we are moving toward the Left, consider the shocking but frighteningly real fact that we have already complied entirely, or in part, with 8 of the 10 planks of Karl Marx's *Communist Manifesto*. Here is just a sampling:

*1. Abolition of property in land and application of...land to public purposes.*
*2. A heavy progressive or graduated income tax.*
*3. Abolition of all right of inheritance.*
*4. Confiscation of the property of all emigrants....*
*5. Centralization of credit in the hands of the State, by means of a*

*national bank with State capital and an exclusive monopoly.*
*6. Centralization of the means of communication and transport*
*in the hands of the State...*[6]

And consider the following facts: already the state, using the Racketeer-Influenced Corrupt Organizations (RICO) statues and administrative decrees that circumvent constitutional rules, has arrogated the "right" to search and seize the properties of citizens, including the offices of physicians, and to impound records, charts and confidential information based on mere allegations and accusations (not convictions) of the dubious charge of "fraud and abuse" in violation of the 4th and 15th Amendments;[7] inheritance taxes, already exorbitant, have gone from 50% to 55% in just the first year of Clinton's presidency; existence of the Federal Reserve with immense central powers and an exclusive monetary monopoly with the prerogative to decide the worth of paper money (and the existance and degree of inflation) at any given time, as there are no standards;[8] the existence of virtual government monopolies, such as Amtrak and Con Rail, and the Federal Communication Commission (FCC) which regulates the airwaves;[9] and then there is the issue of the wetlands which, on the guise of protecting the environment, regulates private property usage—according to the Army Corps of Engineers' manual, soil wetness as detected by a hygrometer placed 18 inches underground for seven days out of a year satisfies the definition of a "wetland," and therefore, is subject to Federal government "protection"—you get the idea, no doubt, which way we are headed...and it is not in the Right direction (**jeu de mots** intended).

We do have our job cut out for us. We have the doubly-daunting task of fighting to preserve the private practice of medicine, avoid socialization, and repel the threatening looming menace of total government takeover, while at the same time educating the public to the realities of America's health care system—the best in the world. Somehow we must awaken our patients from the seductive but treacherous illusion of "free" health care, for there is no free lunch, and dissuade them away from the entitlement mentality affliction transmitted to them as a contagion from leftward liberal politicians and statism-infected health care "experts."

To accomplish this objective, it will be essential that practicing physicians jolt their patients back to reality and break the seductive spell of the socialist sirens. For this task, physicians need to launch a two-prong attack: First, as leading citizens, they must all participate in the health care discussions in their communities, and expose the fallacies of socialized health care, whether government-run or corporate (managed care). Second, as physicians, they must set aside time to educate their patients about the realities of America's health care system and preventive medicine, two issues inextricably entwined. Moreover, space should be allocated in their waiting rooms for pabulum material as consumption for the thought and reflection of their patients. Surprisingly, it seems the majority of physicians, unaware of this tremendous public relation asset (their waiting rooms), do not properly utilize this great resource. I hear that nothing frightens politicians more than physicians talking with and educating their patients about health care issues. A recent article pointed out to me by Jerome C. Arnett, Jr., M.D. of West Virginia encapsulates this truth:

*If all politics is local, the nation's 653,000 physicians are perfectly placed to influence the course of President Clinton's proposed plan as it winds its way through Congress in the coming months. About 3 million Americans enter doctors' offices daily, and many are likely to get an earful of health reform and an eyeful of American Medical Association brochures....The White House isn't represented in doctors' offices, where even proponents of health care reform concede the battle could be won or lost.*[10]

Thus, the health care pundits know physicians have the potential of being able to turn their patients into their greatest and strongest allies—and indeed, in a statewide survey conducted in Georgia in 1993, 85% of Georgians expressed the opinion that they wanted to know what their personal physicians think about health care.[11]

Make no mistake about it, the battle for the survival of the practice of private medicine represents more than just a struggle between two diametrically opposed sectarian factions attempting to dictate the mechanism of health care delivery, even more importantly, philosophically, this struggle symbolizes the titanic conflict between two rival ideologies: one that restores the sanctity of the patient-doctor relationship based on genuine compassion, charity, and trust; respects private contracts and free associations; advocates free-market incentives; espouses liberty with individual responsibility; and recognizes that human nature is such that individuals pursue their self-interest and this usually leads to desirable social outcomes in the marketplace.[12] The alternative, on the other hand, represents an omnipotent government, dictates patient care, mandates coercive compassion, responds only to pressure by special interest groups, and insists on statism and collectivism because its proponents believe that an amoral bureaucracy can do better than the individual in providing for him/herself and his/her family. This is well exemplified in Clinton's ill-fated National Health Board so uncannily reminiscent of Ayn Rand's fictitious, yet prophetic, Unification Board of *Atlas Shrugged*. The struggle is too important to be ignored. Let us not forget Benjamin Franklin's admonition: "They that give up essential liberty to obtain temporary safety deserve neither liberty nor safety."

We should militate relentlessly for the institution of tax-free Medical Savings Accounts (MSAs); catastrophic coverage via high-deductible, portable, insurance; expand (and hopefully, privatize) Medicaid to cover all of those who truly can not presently afford insurance; and derail the litigation juggernaut that is devastating America with sensible tort reform[13] and managed care should assume its share of liability in medical malpractice cases. The introduction of personal incentives, not only to remain healthy, but to save in a tax-free MSA, owned by the individual patient-consumer, are immense, while preserving choice of physician, place of treatment, and individualized treatment plan, with quality not sacrificed on the altar of rationing and cost-containment.

Suffice it to say that if we are not successful in our efforts, our fate will be the catastrophic stumble and inevitable plunge down the bottomless pit of socialized medicine with all its horrors, health care rationing, and perhaps, in the not-too-distant future of a brave new world, government-sanctioned euthanasia—not as acts of self-determination, as proclaimed by leading ethicists but as the ultimate form of rationing. The conflict thus represents a leviathan struggle that physicians and their patients can not afford to lose.

## REFERENCES

1. Rand A. Atlas Shrugged, Signet Books, 1957, pp. 346-347.
2. Bauman M. The dangerous samaritans—how we unintentionally injure the poor. Imprimis 1994;23(1).
3. Faria MA Jr. Crisis in health care delivery—rescuing medicine form the clutches of government. J Med Assoc Ga 1992;81(11): 615-620.
4. Horowitz D. Socialism by any other name. National Review 1992;44(7):30.
5. Faria MA Jr: Domestic economic policy and socialism. The Wayfarer Press, Macon, Georgia, September 1992, pp 2-9.
6. Marx K. The Communist Manifesto, 1848.
7. AAPS News. Are doctors like drug-dealers? AAPS News 1992;48(6). AAPS, 1601 N. Tucson Blvd., Suite 9, Tucson, AZ 85716. 1-800635-1196.
8. McManus JF. The fed retains its power. The New American 1994;10(2):44.
9. Lee RW. Attack of the fairness doctrine. The New American 1994;10(2):5-8.
10. Wolf R, and Hasson J. In Switch; doctors take their case to patients. USA Today, January 24, 1994.
11. Physicians Prescription for Georgia. Report of survey conducted under the aegis of the Medical Association of Georgia, 1993.
12. Goodman JC, and Musgrave GL. Patient Power—The Free Enterprise Alternative to Clinton's Health Plan. CATO Institute, Washington, D.C., 1994.
13. Faria MA Jr. The litigation juggernaut. Part I: The dimensions of the devastation. J Med Assoc Ga 1993;82(8):393-398, and Part II: Strategies and tactics for victory. J Med Assoc Ga 1993;82(9):447-451.

(APRIL, 1994)

# CHAPTER 11

# *PLAYING HARDBALL IN HEALTH CARE REFORM*

## AN INTERESTING PROPHECY

*I recently reread, after 30 years, Ayn Rand's novel* Atlas Shrugged. *As you may recall, Rand's philosophy of objectivism glorifies the individual and disparages politicians and the bureaucracy. The book is about individualists who leave society because "looters" are taking more and more from them. One paragraph relates to a physician. "I quit when medicine was placed under State control, some years ago," said Dr. Hendricks. "Do you know what it takes to perform a brain operation? Do you know the kind of skill it demands, and the years of...devotion that go to acquire that skill? That was what I would not place at the disposal of men whose sole qualifications to rule me was their capacity to spout the fraudulent generalities that got them elected to the privilege of enforcing their wishes at the point of a gun. I would not let them dictate the purpose for which my years of study had been spent, or the conditions of my work, or my choice of patients, or the amount of my reward...in all the discussions that preceded the enslavement of medicine, men discussed everything—except the desire of the doctors. Men considered only the 'welfare' of the patients with no thoughts for those who were to provide it. That a doctor should have any right, desire or choice in the matter, was regarded as irrelevant selfishness; his is not to choose, they said, only 'to serve.' ...I have often wondered at the smugness with which people assert their right to enslave me, to control my work, to force my will, to violate my conscience, to stifle my mind—yet what is it that they expect to depend on, when they lie on an operating table under my hands?...Let them discover, in their operating rooms and hospital wards, that it is not safe to place their lives in the hands of a man whose life they have throttled. It is not safe, if he is the sort of man who resents it—and still less safe, if he is the sort who doesn't."[1]*

This small segment of a great book is very relevant to medicine today. Remember it was published in 1957, before Medicare, Medicaid, and other public policy health care concerns. Today, as in the passage quoted, others are telling physicians and patients what is best, and fewer are seeking guidance from doctors. Policymakers, hospitals, and the insurance industry are developing the rules, and physicians and patients are expected to "come aboard."

> *It seems that, as in* Atlas Shrugged, *the "desire of doctors" to a "right" in the discussion is being ignored. Perhaps we ought to remind those who are contemplating health care policy whom they want in control when they are on the operating room table.*[2]
>
> Martin I. Resnick, M.D.
> Editor-in-Chief, *Contemporary Urology* (January 1994)

Talk about prophetic revelations! Various polls in the last couple of years have indicated a significant number of physicians, especially those over 55, are already thinking about quitting their profession, citing government intrusion, bureaucratic interference, and the litigation crisis as the major reasons for their dissatisfaction with the present system of health care delivery. Additional numbers of physicians would likely be added to the exodus if socialized medicine is instituted—whether in the disingenuous form of managed competition as promoted by the Clintons, or the single-payer system as advocated by Rep. James McDermott (D-WA) and Senator Paul Wellstone (D-MN); in addition, the universal Medicare coverage option has been reintroduced by that restless soul: Rep. Fortney "Pete" Stark (D-CA).

The systems, in which government and bureaucracy feature prominently in health care delivery—managed care with or without global budgets—have been discussed repeatedly in *JAMA*, *NEJM*, and *American Medical News*; we have also spent some time discussing them in the *Journal of the Medical Association of Georgia* in the context of the ongoing debate on health care reform.

As we move toward the right on the spectrum of health care options, we encounter more "moderate" plans in the form of managed competition which differ only in the degrees of iniquity but not in principles from the Clintonian brand of managed competition. Here, we find Representative Jim Cooper's (D-TX) plan, which he has himself styled "Clinton Lite." Instead of *regional alliances* (government cartels), we have *purchasing cooperatives*. Instead of *global budgets* and the *National Health Board*, we hear "competition" as the key for cost controls. The reality is that competition, as in managed competition, is (and remains) an oxymoronic proposition. Managed competition is an unstable entity that will collapse under its own bloated bureaucratic weight, and if fully implemented, will pave the way for socialized medicine in all its purity: the single-payer. Managed competition, with or without global budgets or employer mandates, is the prelude for further government interference, regulation, and ultimately control of the health care industry—the essence of socialized medicine.

In fact, it was the fear of this managed competition monstrosity—and not love for socialized medicine—that apparently pushed the American College of Surgeons (ACS) to endorse, although equivocally, the single-payer system last February. No, it was not passionate love at first sight but fear of the future and preemptive resignation that led to the regrettable misunderstanding by the leadership of the ACS. In fact, Chairman David Murray, M.D., said the ACS leadership "acted out of frustration with insider-run managed care plans and a desire to bring about reform that permits patients to select the physician or surgeon of their choice."[3] Yet, here again, a major national medical organization nearly capitulated without polling its members. Months before, the American Academy of Family Physicians (AAFP) endorsed the Clinton proposal, yet a poll conducted by the American Association of Physicians and Surgeons (AAPS) found that 71% of family physicians are opposed to President Clinton's plan for health care reform.[4] What follows are the names of the organizations which have jumped onto the Clinton bandwagon of socialized medicine:*

• American Academy of Family Physicians—The AAFP has a membership of 74,000. William Coleman, M.D., President of the AAFP, went on MacNeil Lehrer following the AMA vote reaffirming advocacy for the employer mandate.

• American Academy of Pediatrics—The AAP is a member organization of the AMA with a membership of 47,000.

• American College of Obstetricians and Gynecologists—ACOG has a membership of 33,000.

• American College of Physicians—With a membership of 77,000 practitioners of internal medicine, ACP is the largest medical specialty society in the United States. They are a member group of the AMA.

• American College of Preventive Medicine—ACPM has

* Source: *The White House, December 16, 1993. Statements of support on file.*

2,000 members, half of the 4,000 preventive specialists in the United States.

• American Medical Women's Association—The AMWA membership consists of 13,000 women physicians and medical students and is dedicated to promoting women's health and the influence of women in the medical profession.

• American Society of Internal Medicine—ASIM membership is approximately 26,500.

• American Thoracic Society—The ATS is a professional organization of over 11,000 physicians and other health care providers specializing in pulmonary medicine and lung-related research. They are the medical section of the American Lung Association.

• National Medical Association—The NMA is the primary professional medical organization representing 17,000 African-American physicians. Their membership consists primarily of physicians in the primary care specialties.

• National Hispanic Medical Association—The NHMA has a membership of approximately 39,000.

By luring an array of pragmatic leaders of medical organizations, President Clinton was able to claim that 300,000 physicians who belong to those sundry medical organizations have rallied to his cause. He further used these figures by stating that the total membership of these, supportive, organizations exceeds the membership of the AMA. In fact, the rank and file physicians in these organizations were largely unaware of the drastic steps taken by their respective leaders.

Credit should be given where it is due: despite the AMA's indecision regarding employer mandates and other issues, it was one of only two national organizations that has refused to jump aboard the bandwagon of socialized medicine. The other organization is the AAPS, which according to its Executive Director, Jane Orient, M.D., "is the one national medical organization that is unequivocally opposed to socialized medicine on principle...The train is headed over a cliff, and it is our responsibility to turn it around."[5] And indeed, Daniel Johnson, M.D., Speaker of the House of Delegates of the AMA, has acknowledged that "enactment of the Clinton Plan would mean the end of private practice."[4]

Allow me now to return to Ayn Rand's *Atlas Shrugged*, which incidentally, has been proclaimed the most widely read book in America, after the Bible. It is utterly astonishing that even in those seemingly complacent times in the 1950s when physicians believed there was no need for political activism for themselves and their patients, the objectivist philosopher and novelist Ayn Rand's clairvoyance had allowed her to see into the crystal ball and recognize the social, economic, and political changes that were coming down the pipes. She prophesied the unparalleled growth of the federal government, and the regulations, interference, and ultimate control of businesses and industries—including the health care industry, by the self-replicating government bureaucracy. She described how some academicians, incited by professional jealousy and envious of the growth of wealth in the private sector, went along with socialist planning, and in collusion with government policymakers, enviously unleashed onerous regulations to sabotage the growth of private enterprise and capitalism.

Ayn Rand envisioned the formation of an all-powerful, omniscient, government-appointed, bureaucratic entity, *The Unification Board*, which stifled business enterprises; imposed cumbersome regulations; impeded trade, research, and development; trampled upon individual liberties; established draconian wage and price controls; and oversaw all professions, including the medical profession, to make sure they complied with government edicts. In short, as in any authoritarian country, the oppressive, regulatory Board became the destructive fourth branch of government. The Unification Board, in Ayn Rand's novel, had effectively imposed America's own brand of socialism; totalitarianism had been imposed not by revolution but by silent, step-by-step encroachment (evolution). In Ayn Rand's America, businesses crumbled, the populace became cynical and demoralized, taxation became exorbitant, and then...the movers and shakers of society vanished...ultimately chaos reigned. The only ones gloating were those who had heavily and nefariously imbibed on the politics of envy.

Today, the situation has certainly not deteriorated to the lowpoint depicted in *Atlas Shrugged*, but we certainly seem to be headed in that direction. Many stories have run of CEOs and executives (although certainly not those in managed care organizations) resigning their positions of wealth and power to spend "quality time" with their families, and becoming "house-husbands." Eminent statesmen are shunning appointment to high government posts, and even politicians are declining to serve further terms in the House and Senate. Perhaps, nowhere is there more dissatisfaction than in the House of Medicine. Polls, commentaries, and letters to the editors in the various medical publications over the last couple of years demonstrate the growing dissatisfaction with the deteriorating status quo in medicine.

Today's reality is that we are on the verge of transferring 1/7th of the U.S. economy, which constitutes 15% of the U.S. GNP, to the government—all in a single scoop via President Clinton's Health Security Act of 1993. Other Clinton-lite, "more moderate," managed competition (managed care and HMO) schemes at the state level will be conducive to the same end, piecemeal. And, at the center-piece of his proposal stands majestically an imposing *National Health Board*, with dictatorial, administrative powers that would rival those of Ayn Rand's fictitious Unification Board as well as the all-too-powerful and real IRS.* "A hyperbolic statement," you counter. "Not so," I reply. "Read on." The National Health Board (NHB) would be comprised of 7 presidential appointees unaccountable to the public. They would set national health standards and administer the new system. It would interpret, approve, and upgrade what is included in the benefits package and issue regulations. Its regulations would preempt local and state regulations.** The NHB would enforce the budget via the regional health alliances (these are the government-run cartels that would likely be dominated by the big 5: Aetna, Prudential, Travelers, Cigna, Met Life; and, of course, Blue Cross/Blue Shield).

We were told by the First Lady that states would be given

* Incidentally, the IRS remains busy stalking physicians. *AMNews* reports (3/14/94) that the "IRS is searching for doctors' unreported hospital incentives." These incentives may be financial incen-tives, "cash bonuses, guaranteed private incomes, below-market loans, reduced or free office rent, moving expenses, and subsidized health or professional liability insurance."

** I am aware of the statements by the health care pundits to the effect that the NHB will not pass Congress, but I remain deeply skeptical. We must also be vigilant of a cosmetic name change or the formation of another bureaucratic entity in its place, a wolf in sheep's clothing. Since the inception of the Great Society, regulatory agencies have doubled in number every decade; that means the bureaucrats' regulatory powers have grown in geometric proportions in the last three decades.

flexibility, that they would be the laboratories of democracy. The problem is that for those statements to become reality, there is only one road they can follow. The states must throw down the towel and opt for a single-payer system, or adopt a bureaucratic, Clinton-like, managed competition system with price-fixing (global budgets) and built-in rationing mechanisms directed at cost containment.* That is why Elizabeth McCaughey, the John M. Olin Fellow at the Manhattan Institute, wrote in *The New Republic* that there was *no exit* in President Clinton's proposal of managed competition.[7]

The NHB would regulate drug prices and by this act could well end up killing the ground-breaking research and development of life-saving drugs by the American pharmaceutical industry. For the last 40 years, 65% of all life-saving drugs have been researched and developed in the U.S. (Switzerland comes second at nearly 7%).[8]

The NHB would also be charged with reviewing and approving the alliances' plans submitted to the states and the Secretary of Health and Human Services (HHS). HHS would be authorized to withhold federal dollars to states not in compliance while the Secretary of the Treasury would impose "additional payroll taxes on all employers in a state not in compliance."[9] Premiums would be set by community ratings but reflecting "contemporary family structures" and abiding by the budget caps set by the NHB.

The Advisory Council of the NHB would establish a National Quality Management Program which would conduct consumer surveys, set national goals, establish minimal standards, and publish annual performance reports. Quality reports would include data on access appropriateness, outcomes of care, and even satisfaction of care.

The NHB would expand anti-kickback statues covering Medicare and Medicaid to include all third-party payers selected by the regional alliances. Moreover, the NHB would be the final arbiter as to what treatments become "medically necessary" and constitute "quality service." A failure to match the proper diagnosis with the proper treatment guidelines could become a crime.[10] The NHB would decide if treatments that are deemed inappropriate pose a

---

* This technique of allowing reimbursement for only "medically approved" treatments and procedures, along with queues and serial delisting of medical treatments and drugs, are insidious forms of rationing in Canada, which under managed competition, could easily be tailored to fit America's own brand of socialized medicine.[6]

"serious threat" to the public, in which case, treatments would not only be non-covered, but also would empower the office of the Inspector General to commence asset forfeiture proceedings against the provider. In other words, the government would be given the authority "to seize anything you [a physician] own if convicted of a health care offense."[10]

Furthermore, there would be new criminal penalties such as "bribery," when patients seek to pay health care providers for services that are not approved by the NHB. "Providers are subject to civil monetary penalties for a number of offenses including failure to comply with information standards."[11]

The reality is that appeasement—of those who want to enslave the medical profession and transform our health care delivery system from the best in the world to a bureaucratic maze of cost controls and rationing—has not worked. We can delude ourselves that we are "partners" with Big Brother, or that we have "a seat at the table," but the reality is that we have been kept well outside the tent. Unless one lives in fantasy land, the fact remains that despite our cooperation, acquiescence, and complacency, the last few years have not been good for medicine.

We have been under the heavy fusillade of government bureaucrats (and even private third-party payers who have learned to emulate their counterparts in government) and the enfilade of intrepid attorney-litigators. We have truly been under siege. Consider a recent newspaper article which read:

*For decades, some truths of Washington ran this way: If you don't want to be bloodied, don't mess with the gun lobby. Don't tangle with tobacco interests. Don't cross the doctors. And now, gun and tobacco controls are on the books and the doctors are on the run....In decades past, the cry of 'socialized medicine' could kill a bill, but the American Medical Association couldn't stop Medicare in 1965, when Lyndon Johnson made the case for taking care of the health of the uninsured elderly. Now, rather than fight, the AMA has chosen to take a seat at the table on health care reform.*[12]

And, it would appear that the public has come to not trust us (as a profession) because in their eyes we either rally behind politically expedient causes or come out to fight only to protect our economic turf. It is time to counterattack. We owe it to our patients, our families, our country, and ourselves—to become informed and proactive in the debate. With education we can rally the populace behind us. Perhaps an effective strategic counterattack is to demonstrate our earnestness and determination by taking tough political stands based on intellectual integrity and objectivity. We can be compassionate and at the same time remain honest—with our patients, and ourselves. For too long physicians have been content with working hard and long hours, taking care of their patients in the trenches of health care delivery, and remaining quiet and uninvolved. It has not worked. Look at where that complacent policy has taken us: We are about to be swallowed up by the voracious appetite of managed care organizations and HMOs under government authority and monopolistic government protection.

We can no longer afford to sit quietly and idly by while the best health care system in the world, despite its faults, is being vitiated and dismantled. For working hard and long hours, our detractors have called us greedy. For the political expediency of our leaders, we have been mocked and our entreaties rebuffed. And when we have declined to go along with the changes, we have been labeled "a special interest." Enough is enough!

We can no longer take politically correct stands based on pragmatism and expediency and expect to regain the esteem of the public and the respect of our detractors. It is time to regain the esteem of the public or the respect of our detractors. It is time to regain our dignity and respect by taking firm stands on socio-economic and political issues based on principles, balanced by the wishes of our rank and file members, rather than political expediency and acquiescence. Pragmatism has failed us miserably. Let us return to medicine's idealism, and altruism will follow naturally. We have a window of opportunity to regain the trust and respect of the public, not only by reaffirming our position as the patients' true advocates, but also by vigorously defending our profession.

We need to take time from our practices to inform the public about our mission and explain our work. Our efforts can convert a populace eager to learn about health care issues into legions of informed, vigilant citizens who will rally behind our just causes: *patient-oriented, free-market medicine* with truly compassionate care for all, the revivification of the sanctity of the patient-doctor relationship, and the implementation of meaningful medicolegal reforms. As Thomas Jefferson wrote in 1816, "Enlighten the people generally, and tyranny and oppression of body and mind will vanish like evil spirits at the dawn of day." Through the ages, physicians have always done their duty, today let us do ours.

### REFERENCES

1. Rand A. Atlas Shrugged. Random House, New York, 1957, p.744.
2. Resnick MI. An interesting prophecy. Contemp Urol 1994; January:11.
3. McIlrath S. Surgeons back single payer. Am Med News 1994; February 28.
4. AAPS News 1994;50(4):1-4. 1601 N. Tucson Blvd., Suite 9, Tucson, Az. 85716. (800)635-1196.
5. Orient J. Personal communication, March 7, 1994.
6. Goodman WE. Health care in Canada: face-to-face with reality. J Med Assoc Ga 1993;82(12):647-649.
7. McCaughey E. No exit: are you really ready for the Clinton Health Care Plan? The New Republic 1994;February 7:21-25.
8. Pharmaceutical Manufacturers Association. New single chemical entity drugs introduced to the U.S. market 1940-1990. Cited by Francis Davis (Publisher) in Private Practice 1992;24(9):3.
9. Faria MA Jr. On Clinton's health care reform proposals, further reflections. J Med Assoc Ga 1994;83(1):11-14.
10. Young GM. Criminal, quasi-criminal, and medical liability under the Clinton plan. AAPS Legal Supplement, February 1994.
11. Trickle-down medicine. AAPS News 1994;50(3):1-4.
12. Feinsilber M. Untouchables are fair game for legislators—tobacco, doctors, guns are no longer safe. The Associated Press. The Macon Telegraph, April 3, 1994.

(JUNE, 1994)

## Chapter 12

# *Health Care as a Right*

*By physical liberty I mean to do anything which does not interfere with the happiness of another. By intellectual liberty I mean the right to think wrong.*
Robert G. Ingersoll (1833-1899)

*The government is best which governs the least, because its people discipline themselves.*
Thomas Jefferson (1743-1826)

*The average man that I encounter all over the country regards government as a sort of great milk cow, with its head in the clouds eating air, and growing a full teat for everybody on earth.*
Clarence C. Manion

*The law perverted! And the police power of the state perverted along with it! The law, I say, not only turned from its proper purpose! The law becomes the weapon of every kind of greed! Instead of checking crime, the law itself guilty of the evils it is supposed to punish!*
Frederic Bastiat, *The Law* (1850)

Let us trace the history of the evolution of the concept of laws and rights and review the evidence as to whether or not such a right to medical care exists.

The concept of rights evolved from English political philosophy that began with the signing of the Magna Carta in 1215 and subsequently expounded upon by such champions of liberty as Sir Edward Coke (1552-1634), Sir William Blackstone (1723-80), and John Locke (1632-1704). Locke believed all men were equal and **free to pursue** "life, health, liberty and possessions."[1] The government of a state was formed by a social contract with the people it governed, and this social contract was guided by natural law which in turn, guaranteed that those unalienable rights, belonging to all citizens, were not trampled upon by the monopolistic power of government. In the same light, John Locke wrote in 1690: "Every man has a property in his own person. This nobody has any right to but he himself. The labor of his body and the work of his hands are properly his."[2]

Our philosopher-president, Thomas Jefferson, borrowed ideas from, and was indebted to these gentlemen, particularly John Locke, for his concept of natural rights. Jefferson expanded on the concept of natural rights in the political document **par excellence**, when he wrote:

*We hold these truths to be self-evident, that all men are created equal, that they are endowed by their Creator with certain unalienable Rights, that among these, are Life, Liberty and the pursuit of Happiness. That, to secure these rights, Governments are instituted among men, deriving their just Powers from the consent of the governed.*

The framers of the U.S. Constitution were wary of the power which even they had themselves created during the Federal Constitutional Convention of 1787. Therefore, to further protect the personal liberties of the people from usurpation by government, they later added the Bill of Rights, the first ten amendments to the Constitution. And thus, along these same lines, James Madison (1751-1836; 4th President of the U.S. 1809-17) wrote: "I believe there are more instances of the abridgement of the freedom of the people by gradual and silent encroachments of those in power than by violent and sudden usurpations."[3]

It is doubtful that the U.S. Constitution would have been ratified in 1789 if a promise of adoption of a Bill of Rights had not been made. Thomas Jefferson, who was in Paris serving as U.S. Minister to France at the time of the Constitutional Convention, praised many of the features of the proposed constitution but lamented the lack of a Bill of Rights.[4]

### LIFE, LIBERTY, AND PROPERTY

The 5th Amendment, in addition to propounding the criminal defense rights, also protects the natural rights of citizens, so that they could not be "deprived of life, liberty or property without due process of law; nor shall private property be taken for public use, without just compensation."

The 13th Amendment of 1865 ended slavery and involuntary servitude, while the 14th Amendment of 1868 was intended to end the after-effects of slavery in the South and included a clause providing that no state shall "deprive any person of life, liberty or property, without due process of law; nor deny to any person within its jurisdiction of the equal protection of the law"—which in effect incorporates and applies the doctrine and protection of the Bill of Rights of the individual to states. The 5th, 13th, and 14th Amendments afford constitutional protections for the Natural or God-given rights previously delineated by John Locke and the Declaration of Independence.

Civil rights are "the nonpolitical rights of a citizen, especially those guaranteed by the 13th and 14th Amendments to the Constitution and by acts of Congress."[5] This simple definition, likewise, reiterates the fact that unadulterated civil rights derive from natural rights because they liberate the individual from bondage and allow him to pursue his life's interest and to maximize his life's potential. The last clause, namely, "and by acts of Congress," unfortunately, has opened the door for the creation of a veritable menu of unenumerated rights, including welfare rights. Ignorance has compounded the problem. For example, a 1987 survey by the Hearst Corporation found that only 41% of Americans knew that the Bill of Rights was comprised of the first 10 amendments to the U.S. Constitution; 75% incorrectly believed that the Constitution guarantees the right to free public education, and 42% believed that the document guarantees every citizens the right to health care for those who cannot afford it.[6]

Natural rights are akin to human rights. They are the rights to life, liberty, property, and the pursuit of happiness and one's life interests and avocations without interference from others, as long as those actions do not infringe on the rights of others. The enumerated rights in the Bill of Rights were drafted as to abide by the important concept—viz, that the process of natural rights connects the concepts of civil liberties, individual autonomy, and the negative concepts of laws.

Professor Charles E. Rice of Nortre Dame Law School believes that "a legally enforceable right is either positive or natural. A positive right exists only because it is created by a constitution, statute or other forms of positive law."[7] Natural (human) rights, embodying the negative concept of laws, are not granted by the state, for they are inherent to human beings. The state merely guarantees and enforces them.

According to the framers, these basic rights are, in turn, protected by a vigilant citizenry by the exercise of the 2nd Amendment, if the need ever arises. That is what James Madison, the "master builder of the Constitution" and also the author of the 2nd Amendment, meant when he wrote, "the advantage that the Americans have over every other nation is that they are armed." James Madison believed the reason governments of other countries disarmed their citizens was because they recognized their tendency to accumulate power (and to degenerate into despotism); therefore, those governments did not trust their own people to own guns to protect their liberties.[3] It is therefore no wonder that the right "to keep and bear arms" has been called by writer, Robert W. Lee, "the right that secures all others."[8]

The rights to life, liberty, and property (meaning the right to own or dispose of property as one sees fit) are the classical examples of natural rights, basic rights which are inherent to a person and do not infringe on another person's rights. The problem with positive rights, on the other hand, is that they are granted by the government and therefore are subject to the whims of the state and the blowing winds of political expediency. Thus, subject to the foibles of human nature, they may be arbitrary and unjust, and encroach upon other individuals' basic rights. Moreover, there is still the problem that what the state gives, it can also take away. Natural rights and basic human rights transcend the state and are derived directly from "God or Nature."

As Professor Rice points out, St. Thomas Aquinas (1225-1274), the Italian theologian and medieval philosopher, recognized the fact that if human law "deflects from the law of nature, it is unjust and is no longer a law but a perversion of law."[7] And the Roman stoic philosopher and orator, Cicero (106-43 B.C.), who did not believe in a Judeo-Christian God, but recognized natural law, predicated that the power of the state be limited. He wrote:

*[W]hat is right and true is also eternal, and does not begin or end with written statutes....From this point of view it can*

*be readily understood that those who formulated wicked and
unjust statutes for nations, thereby breaking their promises and
agreements, put into effect anything but "laws." It may thus be
clear that in the very definition of the term "law" there inheres the
idea and principle of choosing what is just and true....Therefore
Law is the distinction between things just and unjust, made in
agreement with that primal and most ancient of all things,
Nature; and in conformity to nature's standard are framed those
human laws which inflict punishment upon the wicked but
defend and protect the good.*[7]

Moreover in our own American Republic, Alexander
Hamilton (1755-1804), the American patriot who led the heroic
charge against the entrenched British at Yorktown in 1781, asserted,
"No tribunal, no codes, no systems can repeal or impair this law of
God, for by His eternal laws it is inherent in the nature of things."[7]

"Traditional legal rights," according to Professor Iredell
Jenkins of the University of Alabama Law School, "are primarily
protective: they guarantee citizens certain basic freedoms and
immunities, and protect them against intrusion or arbitrary action
by the state. These rights do not bestow any positive benefits upon
the people...these traditional rights are not conferred on citizens by
the state; rather, the people hold these rights prior to and indepen-
dently of the state, which is merely enjoined to respect them and
assure their free exercise."[9]

Is medical care a genuine basic right? I don't think so. Let
me explain further. In my estimation, health care, or the right to
medical care is not a right, just as there are no such rights as to
shelter (housing), clothing, food, or for that matter, a two-week
all-paid vacation to Cancun, Mexico, or any other exotic *panem et
circenses*. One only has the right to *pursue* those goals.

In essence, no individual is entitled to the services or the
fruits of another's labor without just compensation. Physicians
should be free to offer their services free of government coercion
and, at least in theory, on whatever terms he or she chooses. As
Objectivist philosopher, David Kelley, points out:

*"A right is a principle that specifies something which an
individual should be free to have or do. A right is an entitlement,
something one possesses free and clear, something one can exer-*

*cise without asking anyone else's permission. Since it is not a privilege or favor, we do not owe anyone else any gratitude for their recognition of our rights.*

*"But there is no such right [to Medical care].There cannot be—not in a free society which recognizes the genuine rights of individuals to their own autonomy."*[11]

Nevertheless, the truth is that counterfeit rights are being added at an alarming rate to the ever-expanding menu of government entitlements, (i.e., welfare rights), to placate powerful special interests and favored sundry minority groups.This menu has been (and continues to be) expanded and encumbered on the shoulders of the citizenry, the American taxpayer.[12] And for those who say that the Constitution authorizes federal welfare programs (welfare "rights") let me quote two of the Founding Fathers who knew better.Thomas Jefferson, in discussing whether Congress had such an authority, wrote: "a distinct substantive power, to do any act which might tend to the general welfare, is to render all the enumerations [of their specific constitutional powers] useless, and to make their power unlimited."[13] And James Madison, in a letter to Edmund Pendleton dated January 21, 1792, wrote:"[If] Congress can do whatever in their discretion can be done by money, and will promote the General Welfare, the Government is no longer a limited one, possessing enumerated powers, but an indefinite one, subject to particular exceptions."[13]

The drive behind this voracious appetite for the creation of the assortment of welfare and special interest group rights is the subtle but populist, priggish yet seductive, lure of socialism.The end result is that government is creating rights and automatic entitlements, *pari passu*, with the creation of dependency and oppression. Historical evidence is clear: when government goes beyond basic rights and civil liberties (e.g., individual freedom, the freedom to think and act privately, without hindrance from government), the specter of tyranny looms over the populace. True basic (human) rights are either God-given or Nature-derived and guaranteed by a just constitutional government, with clearly limited powers. Such are the natural (human) rights as declared in the Declaration of Independence, namely, life, liberty and the pursuit of happiness, the constitutional rights enumerated in the Bill of Rights, and the civil rights guaranteed in the 13th, 14th, 15th, and 19th Constitutional Amendments, as well as the Civil Right Acts of 1878 and the portions of the 1964 Act guaranteeing desegregation and equality of opportunity. Once government transcends those rights, it squarely infringes upon the rights of the people and the negative concept of the law. The negative concept of the law is desirable because law in its essence is force.

The French statesman, Frederic Bastiat (1801-1850), in his monumental book, *The Law*, first published in 1850 as a pamphlet, (only two years after Marx's *Communist Manifesto*), explains the basic right of an individual to be left alone by the state to pursue life, liberty and property, as long as he does not infringe upon the rights of others.[14] As stated by Bastiat, the purpose of the law is to prevent injustice, not the "creation of peace through the elimination of poverty," as recently asserted by Professor Daniel Maguire and Dr. Edith McFadden.[15] Bastiat wrote that the law keeps a person within the balance of justice and imposes nothing upon the individual, but a mere negation of unjust actions. "[The laws] oblige him only to abstain from harming others. They violate neither his personality, his liberty, nor his property. They safeguard all of these. They are defensive; they defend equally the rights of all." Moreover, "...when the law, by means of its necessary agent, force, imposing upon men a regulation of labor, and method or subject of education or religious faith or creed—then the law is no longer negative. It acts positively upon people. It substitutes the will of the legislature for their own will."[14]

In short, I contend that when the services or labor of one person (as in the practice of competent and compassionate medicine by a physician) or one's property taken (as in the application of asset forfeiture laws to physicians accused, not convicted of any wrongdoing) is taken by the state, then we are not dealing with rights or justice or philanthropy, but legalized plunder, institutionalized servitude, oppression, and injustice.

A right to medical care imposes an obligation on a physician to provide a service to a stranger with whom he/she has not even established a patient-doctor relationship. And you ask, "What about those who cannot pay for their health care?"

My answer: Indigent patients have always been taken care of by the medical profession with dignity and compassion, because physicians have always provided charity care, **pro bono**. In fact, one issue that is not given proper attention by the media is the charity and uncompensated care provided by American physicians. A recent AMA survey showed that American physicians provide $11 billion of uncompensated care (or an average of 150 hours of care annually, free of charge). Specifically, data from California shows that $50,000 of uncompensated care is provided per physician either *pro bono publico* or governmentally mandated in that state. This figure appears no different from that in other states.[16]

And before government began its mandates, physicians were happy to provide indigent care as something that came with their territory—just as long hours and getting calls in the middle of the night—something that came with the privilege of being a member of a compassionate, venerable profession, a profession financially remunerated commensurately with the value of services rendered (the best care in the world).

Apparently that was not enough for government bureaucrats, self-styled health experts, and biomedical ethicists who did not want to accept the idea (and therefore wanted to establish the fact) that when a physician gets up in the middle of the night to provide a charitable emergency room service—that the patient does not owe him/her gratitude. And indeed, if medical care is a right, then the patient owes the physician nothing.

In any case, all of this seems to be now only an intellectual exercise, an academic argument, a Socratic dialogue. Many Americans are convinced of the necessity of the general population to subsidize the medical care of those who can not afford it (or who are just plain not willing to pay for it). And that is fine. But then, the government and the public should pay fair market value for those medical services to compensate for the fruits of a physicians' labors—fruits which, as time marches by, are plucked from the physicians' labor tree without proper compensation and without their permission. If in doubt, review the events of the last 3 decades: the inception and expansion of Medicare and Medicaid which has brought the imposition of arbitrary price controls and, at least in the case of Medicare, has also applied a barrage of coercion and intimidation tactics, and the concept of RBRVS, a concept derived from the Marxist theory of labor and values. By the brute force of administrative law, government authorities (i.e., HHS and HCFA) have imposed a strangle hold of rules and oppressive regulations (i.e., OSHA, CLIA, ADA, etc.); have forced unconstitutional laws (i.e., *ex post facto* laws); have enacted civil and criminal asset forfeiture statutes, treating physicians as if they were drug dealers. These criminal proceedings, initially intended against drug dealers, are now universally applied against honest physicians who make honest mistakes (i.e., coding and billing). As if to underscore this fact, health care costs, in the public sector, have continued to escalate, whereas in the private sector, it has flattened out...but that is another story.

In short, medical care as a right would require physicians to provide their services while violating their professional code of free association and negating their legal prerogative to participate in voluntary binding agreements—the professional and legal basis for the establishment of the patient-doctor relationship. It would also set the precedent that he or she will be bound by whatever standards are set by the state. This action not only infringes upon a physician's autonomy, but also, as Frederic Bastiat asserted over a century ago, constitutes legal plunder and organized injustice. The physician becomes an indentured servant bound to the state. Moreover, the patient owes the physician no gratitude for his/her labors because they are entitled by right to his/her labors.

If the state genuinely wants universal coverage, quality health care and freedom of choice, then it should provide the proper, free-market, voluntary incentives for both patients and doctors to pursue those goals without violating the autonomy of either the patient or the doctor, the sanctity and trust of the patient-doctor relationship, or the honor of a noble and venerable profession.

### REFERENCES

1. The Columbia Encyclopedia. Franklin Electronic Publisher, Inc., The Columbia University Press, 1991.
2. Locke J. Two Treatises of Government, 1690.
3. Hamilton A, Madison J, and Jay J. The Federalist Papers. New American Library, New York. Reprinted 1961.
4. Eidsmore J. The Bill of Rights—securing that which is God-given. The New

American 1991;26(7):21-28.

5. The New Merriam-Webster Dictionary. Springfield, Massachusetts, U.S.A., 1989.

6. The Hearst Corporation survey of 1987 cited by Dr. John Eidsmore in The New American, op. cit.

7. Rice CE. Gifts from God—basic rights transcend the state! The New American, May 3, 1993.

8. Lee RW. The right that secures all others. The New American, September 21, 1992.

9. Jenkins I. The concept of rights and the competence of courts. American Journal of Jurisprudence 1973 cited by Rice CE, op. cit.

10. Physician's Prescription for Georgia—Building a Better State of Health. Medical Association of Georgia, July 1993.

11. Kelley D. Is medical care a right? View from the RIGHT. J Med Assoc Ga 1993; 82(11).

12. Will GF. Too much of a good thing. Newsweek, September 23, 1991.

13. T. Jefferson and J. Madison quoted by Robert W. Lee in Collectivist cliche's. The New American, July 13, 1992.

14. Bastiat F. The Law (1850). Reprinted by The Foundation for Economic Education, Inc. (1990), Irvington-On-Hudson, New York, 10533.

15. Maguire DC, and McFadden EA. Is medical care a right. View from the LEFT. J Med Assoc Ga 1993; 82(11).

16. Faria MA Jr. Crisis in health care delivery—rescuing medicine from the clutches of government. J Med Assoc Ga 1992; 81(11):615-620.

(DECEMBER, 1993)

# PART FOUR: THE ROLE OF PUBLIC HEALTH

# Chapter 13

# Guns and Violence

*Free government rests on free men armed, while basic to tyranny is mistrust of the people; hence they deprive them of arms.*
Aristotle (4th Century B.C.)

*They that give up essential liberty to obtain a little temporary safety deserve neither liberty nor safety.*
Benjamin Franklin (1759)

*Today...a dainty and delicate woman, with courage and determination, is more than the equal of any brute who ever trampled the sands of a Roman arena. The difference is a firearm.*
Robert J. Kukla, *Gun Control*

As concerned citizens and caring physicians, we should applaud the efforts and activities of organized medicine that strive to stamp out child abuse and family violence.

With that well-deserved and panegyric introduction said, we must move to another issue intricately related to the issue of domestic and street violence; that is, the issue of gun control. The faulty *post hoc ergo propter hoc* reasoning, "after it therefore because of it," blames guns on the rise of crime and violence in America. Let me bring forth some facts that may shed some light on this issue.

As a neurosurgeon who spent incalculable hours in the middle of the night treating victims of gunshot wounds, and as a person who shares humane and compassionate feelings towards my fellow human being, I deplore the rising violence and crime in America—but the blame must be laid where it belongs. As physicians, we must base our opinions, objections, and recommendations on objective data and scientific facts rather than on emotions or expediency. We, as scientists and humanitarians, owe the public truth and objectivity. Moreover, as the Persian proverb quips, "the man who speaks the truth is always at ease."

It is not myth but a truism corroborated by experience as

well as by objective data that indiscriminate gun control disarms the law-abiding citizens while it does not prevent criminals and street thugs from perpetrating crimes on unwary victims. To underscore this truth, let me share with you some startling statistics that are not usually discussed by the mainstream media or the medical journals.

Less than 2% of crimes committed with firearms are carried out by law-abiding citizens. The vast majority of criminals obtain their guns illegally, which is not difficult since there is already an estimated 65 to 70 million handguns in circulation and 200 million guns of all types.[1]

A ban on gun ownership would not only be unconstitutional but also impossible to execute. As Abraham Lincoln stated, "he who molds public sentiment goes deeper than he who enacts statutes or pronounces decisions. He makes statutes or decisions possible or impossible to execute."

R.W. Lee reports that there are approximately 500,000 police officers in the United States. Thus, assuming three 8-hour shifts and other circumstances (vacations, leaves, etc.), there would only be 125,000 police on duty at any given time to protect a population of 250 million.[2] Moreover, the duty of police officers is not to prevent crime (they cannot), but to apprehend criminals and bring them to justice—*after* a crime has been committed. They cannot be in all places at all times. Furthermore, contrary to popular belief, the police do not have a legal duty to protect the public against criminals.

I have intimated one reason why this is not feasible, and the events of last year's riots in Los Angeles confirmed this truth. Law-abiding citizens had to protect their lives and their properties with guns, particularly, "assault weapons." In fact, according to a 1982 ruling, "there is no constitutional right to be protected by the state against being murdered by criminals or madmen. The constitution...does not require the federal government or the state to provide services, even so elementary a service as maintaining law and order."[3]

What this amounts to is that the state has no legal responsibility to protect citizens from crime; this is a paramount reason why law-abiding citizens must preserve their constitutional right "to keep and bear arms." As citizens, we must assume some responsibility to protect ourselves from the thugs and criminals amongst us.

And here is another handful of pearls: According to Dr. Gary Kleck, Associate Professor of Criminology at Florida State University, "citizens acting in self-defense kill about three times more assailants and robbers than do police." Dr. Kleck found 645,000 defensive uses of handguns by citizens compared with 581,000 criminal misuses of handguns. Thus, *firearms are used more frequently by law-abiding citizens to repel crime than by criminals to perpetrate crime.* Furthermore, "firearms (including handguns) are used another 215,000 times each year to defend against dangerous animals, i.e., snakes, rabid skunks, etc."[4]

Therefore, it should not be surprising that in a survey of 1800 prison inmates, 81% agreed that a smart criminal tries to find out if his potential victim is armed, 74% said that burglars avoid houses when people are home because they fear being shot, and 34% admit to having been scared off, shot at, wounded or even captured by armed citizens.[5]

Furthermore, National Victims Data suggest that "while victims resisting with knives, clubs, or bare hands are about twice as likely to be injured as those who submit, victims who resist with a gun *are only half as likely* to be injured as those who put up no defense." Similarly, regarding women and self-defense, "among those victims using handguns in self-defense, 66% of them were successful in warding off the attack and keeping their property. Among those victims using non-gun weapons, only 40% were successful. Among those victims fleeing the scene, only 35% were successful. Among those victims invoking physical force, only 22% were successful. Among those using verbal shouting, only 20% were successful." The gun is the great equalizer for women when they are accosted in the street or when they are defending themselves and their children at home.[4] Depriving them of the most effective means of self defense only helps criminal predators perpetrate their crimes.

Women continue to be targets of crime. According to a survey by William Barnhill of *The Washington Post*, "73% of all women now over the age of 12 will be victimized, more than a third of them raped, robbed, or assaulted at some point in their lives." But they are fighting back, at least 12 million women now own handguns. Thus, according to Tracey Martin, former manager of the National Rifle Association's Education and Training Division, "a gun can make the difference between being the victim or the victor in a confrontation with a criminal." And Paxton Quigley, who once advocated gun control but now recommends that women learn to protect themselves with handguns, states, "guns in the hands of women who know how to use them do deter crime."[6]

A word about "assault weapons" is also in order. True assault weapons are fully automatic military weapons which are already regulated by federal law. According to Larry Pratt, Executive Director of Gun Owners of America, firearms that are covered under the so-called assault weapons laws are semi-automatic firearms which include some hunting rifles and shotguns which are mechanically indistinguishable from military weapons. Legislation banning these firearms would effectively penalize many hunters (including physician-sportsmen) who are not aware of this fact and believe their hunting rifles and shotguns are exempted.

It should also be noted that handguns, ordinary shotguns, and hunting rifles, not the so-called paramilitary or "assault" weapons, are the firearms most frequently used in domestic violence and street crimes. In fact, Edward Ezell, Curator of the Smithsonian Institute and National Firearms Collection, testified to the Senate Judiciary Committee in 1989 that the "12-gauge shotguns and the .38-caliber revolvers continue to be the primary firearms used in crimes and shootings."[7] Therefore, if draconian gun control measures are instituted, law-abiding citizens would also lose their constitutionally protected right to own guns, whether for hunting purposes or for protection.[7]

The correct approach to gun violence should not involve penalyzing the law-abiding citizens and infringing on his right "to keep and bear arms." Serious attempts to decrease violence committed with firearms should involve keeping guns away from minors (to prevent accidental shootings), and most importantly, convicted felons and criminals who have forfeited their right to possess guns.

In fact, the majority of murderers are career criminals. The typical murderer has a prior criminal history of at least 6 years with four major arrests in his record.[7] There are 20,000 gun laws on the books throughout the states that cover the above restrictions. They need to be enforced—they are not.

More laws are not the answer, except perhaps for the promotion of instantenous checks. Using computerized tracking mechanisms, such checks research the background of the individual intending to purchase a firearm. This is a step in the right direction, to be welcomed by the citizenry, as it would deter gun sales to felons and career criminals.

Waiting periods are another story. In states where waiting periods have been instituted, there has been no noticeable decrease in gun availability to criminals nor a decrease in violent crime rates. There have been lurid tales of citizens who have been killed by attackers while waiting to pick up newly-purchased guns. Gun Owners of America keeps track and already has a list of victims in this category. So where does the blame lie?

There is a crisis of conscience in America. There is a trend to absolve the guilty individual of personal responsibility and accountability, and instead, to blame society for every illness and affliction. As a result, by default, society assumes responsibility and accountability on behalf of the individual. It is in this atmosphere that draconian gun control measures have been instituted in Washington DC, New York, and Maryland.

A tougher criminal justice system without revolving prison doors and a larger dose of individual moral responsibility and accountability are needed to reduce domestic violence as well as crime in the streets of America. As physicians, we should encourage better communication and understanding between parents and their children, militate for better education in our schools, and instill social responsibility to reduce illegitimacy and teenage pregnancy. Strongly needed are principles of moral and spiritual guidance that encourage family cohesiveness.

As physicians, we should be involved in efforts to reduce domestic violence and street crime. Our guidance should be, nevertheless, buttressed by truth and scientific methodology tempered by the compassion worthy of our profession. But, this does not mean that we should let the emotional aspect of domestic crime and street violence lead us to give up our natural right to liberty or our (and our patients') right as citizens "to keep and bear arms," as guaranteed by the Second Amendment to the U.S. Constitution. We should not support draconian gun control measures that would disarm the law-abiding citizens and leave them to the mercy of criminals who have guns. Giving lip service to political correctness and joining the bandwagon of political expediency or contemporary trends to ingratiate ourselves with the media are not the answer, nor are they worthy of the trust bestowed upon our profession.

### REFERENCES

1. Gottlieb AM. Gun Rights Fact Book, 1988.
2. Lee RW. Going for our guns. The New American, 1990.
3. U.S. Court of Appeals for the Seventh Circuit. *Bowers v. DeVito*.
4. Kleck G. Point Blank—Guns and Violence in America. New York, Aldine de Gruyter, 1991.
5. Blackman PH. The armed criminal in America. New Dimensions, April 1991.
6. Quigley P. Armed and Female, 1992.
7. Kates DB Jr, and Harris PT. How to make their day. National Review 1991;43(9):30-32.

(JULY, 1993)

CHAPTER 14

# *MEDICINE AND GUN CONTROL*

*And the said Constitution be never construed to authorize Congress...to prevent the people of the United States who are peaceable citizens, from keeping their own arms.*
Samuel Adams (1722-1803)

*On every question of construction [of the Constitution] let us carry our-selves back to the time when the Constitution was adopted, recollect the spirit manifested in the debate, and instead of trying what meaning may be squeezed out of the text, or invested against it, conform to the probable one in which it was passed.*
Thomas Jefferson (1743-1826)

As physicians, we have a moral duty and a professional obligation to stand for intellectual integrity, truth, and objectivity, and it is because of these ennobling qualities that we have undertaken to discuss in these pages the controversial topic of the constitutional right "to keep and bear arms" and citizen self-protection. This topic is particularly relevant because this right, which secures all others, is being eroded by media hype and sensationalism. Moreover, the issues of firearms and violence have now been linked to the U.S. health care reform—both in terms of its effects on health care costs, and morbidity and mortality statistics.

As it turns out, both the impact of gun ownership by law-abiding citizens (for self-protection) and its purportedly adverse relationship to the American health care system take a diametrically opposed perspective (from what one hears and reads from the biased media coverage and distorted television sensationalism), when analyzed critically.

Moreover, we have a responsibility to society, as physicians, to consider this issue intellectually and dispassionately, considering also the bigger picture—namely, that firearms in the hands of the law-abiding may actually be extremely beneficial for the preservation of a free society.

We cannot dodge this issue now that the AMA has made

pronouncements on various stands on gun control. As physicians, we will be asked for advice by influential policymakers and legislators, and we can only be worthy of this trust if we have a stated and well defended position that conveys an objective and wise opinion based on scientific data and sound scholarship.

## GUNS AND THE SECOND AMENDMENT

The Founding Fathers held that man's constitutional rights were God-given and unalienable. Although the government was the guarantor of those rights, it was ultimately on the people themselves that those unalienable rights rested. The informed citizenry were to be the ultimate enforcers, and the Second Amendment was to be the vehicle by which this right was to safeguard and secure all others. You see, the Founding Fathers mistrusted the monopolistic tendency of government to accumulate power at the expense of the rights of the citizenry, and as they put it, "degenerate into despotism."

Well read and well aware of the lessons of history, they also were keenly aware of Aristotle's axiom that free government rested on free men. James Madison, the author of the Second Amendment, wrote, "The advantage that Americans have over every other nation is that they are armed." And the Virginia patriot Patrick Henry, who ardently proclaimed, "Give me liberty or give me death," worked assiduously to incorporate the Bill of Rights into the Constitution and wrote, "The great objective is that every man be armed; everyone who is able may have a gun."

As if to underscore that fact, the same Congress that passed the Bill of Rights (with the Second Amendment) also passed the Militia Act of 1790 which defined the militia as "every able-bodied man of military age." More recently, in the *U.S. v. Verdugo* decision of 1990, the Supreme Court held that when the phrase, "the people" is used in the context of the Second Amendment, it means "individuals"—as to mean "the right of the people to keep and bear arms shall not be infringed."

If we look further back in the pages of history, we find that it was the Lord Protector Oliver Cromwell (1599-1658) who first tried unsuccessfully to disarm the English colonists in America on the grounds that the Commonwealth Army already provided for the common defense, precluding the need for arms in the civilian population ("the militia"). The Founding Fathers, needless to say, never embraced that concept.

And here, in my view, is the strongest argument of all for the right of all law-abiding citizens to be able to "keep and bear arms": The Bill of Rights, in its entirety, was added to the Constitution to limit the power of government; and individual rights were enumerated in this document, so that they would be specifically protected from the monopolistic tendency of government to wrest power away from the individual citizenry.

Like it or not, to assert that the phrase "the people" implied a collective right which, when coupled with the locution "well regulated militia" restricted the meaning of the Second Amendment to a state "militia" of citizen-soldiers, as in the National Guard, is preposterous. If that were the case, the Second Amendment would stand out, alone, as the only amendment in the Bill of Rights that does not stand for individual liberties and as a bulwark against government power—in stark contrast to the other nine amendments, all of which limit the scope and power of government, and protect and enhance the individual rights of citizens.

In short, gun control activists want to implement draconian gun control measures, step-by-step, until they reach their true and ultimate goal: prohibition and confiscation of guns by law-abiding citizens. They know that to do so lawfully and constitutionally, they would need to repeal the Second Amendment, and since they know that they are not strong enough right now to do that, they are going about it in this fashion: media hype, sensationalism, and indoctrination so as to mold public opinion toward step-by-step prohibition. The Brady Bill is not the end of gun control; it is only the beginning. As things now stand, with many of our populace distracted with *panum et circenses* and enamored with economic security at the expense of freedom, repeal of the Second Amendment may not even be needed by those who conspire against liberty, for as the British statesman Edmund Burke wrote in 1790, "The only thing necessary for the triumph of evil is for good men to do nothing."

(MARCH, 1994)

# CHAPTER **15**

# *PUBLIC HEALTH AND GUN CONTROL*

*Laws that forbid the carrying of arms...disarm only those who are neither inclined nor determined to commit crimes...such laws make things worse for the assaulted and better for the assailant; they serve rather to encourage than to prevent homicide, for an unarmed man may be attacked with greater confidence than an armed man.*

> Thomas Jefferson quoting the 18th Century Italian criminologist Cesare Beccaria in *On Crimes and Punishment*, 1764.

In 1991, when the American Medical Association (AMA) launched a major campaign against domestic violence, I, as an active member of organized medicine, joined in this campaign. It was thus while researching the topic of violence that I came to the inescapable conclusion and appalling reality that the medical literature on guns and self-protection had failed to objectively discuss both sides of this issue. And this, despite the purported safeguards of peer-review, the alleged claims to objectivity, and the assurances of integrity in public health and scientific research.

What I found, over the next 4 years, particularly as editor of the *Journal of the Medical Association of Georgia*, was, frankly, that when it came to the issue of violence, guns, and self-protection— most medical journals had taken the easy way out of the *mêlée*. Instead of providing a balanced and fair approach based on truth and objectivity, the medical literature echoed the emotionalism and rhetoric of the mass media. In some cases, it provided politicized pseudo-research to reach predetermined outcomes that bolstered the agenda of the gun control lobby. More recently, they have willfully and intentionally transmogrified the right to keep and bear arms into a public health issue so that the natural right embodied in the Second Amendment may be effectively circumvented by government (public health) fiats.

This view—viz, that gun control is a public health issue rather than one aspect of criminology—espouses the erroneous concept of guns and bullets as virulent pathogens that need to be stamped out by limiting gun availability, and ultimately, eradicating guns from the law-abiding citizenry. They chose to neglect the fact that guns and bullets are inanimate objects that do not follow Koch's Postulates of Pathogenicity, and that behind every shooting there is a person pulling the trigger—and who should be held accountable. This is, in reality, a campaign orchestrated by gun prohibitionists and proponents of big government who are willing to exploit our understandable concern for street violence and sensationalized crime statistics to advance their statist agenda: An ever-increasing government authority, domestic socialism, and the virtual emascula- tion of constitutional government, that, in the final analysis, can come about only by total citizen disarmament.

Despite a surfeit of scientific and epidemiologic studies in the sociologic, legal, and criminologic literature that discuss the benefits of firearm possession by law-abiding citizens—physicians and the general public are not being informed about this information, either by the medical or the lay press. In other words, liberal bias and/or political expediency had censured this most vital information from physicians and the public. As editor of a premier state medical journal, I felt (and still feel) a deep sense of moral duty and professional obligation to inform my medical colleagues about the other side of this issue which had been censored by the main- stream press and, regretably, by our own medical establishment.

The monolithic wall of censorship of the entrenched political medical establishment was finally breached in the widely read series of articles and editorials published in the January, March, and May 1994 issues of the *Journal of the Medical Association of Georgia*. In those issues, Professor Gary Kleck of Florida State University, author of the influential book, *Point Blank: Guns and Violence in America* (1991) and Dr. Edgar Suter, National Chair of Doctors for Integrity in Research and Public Policy critically analyzed the work of Dr. Arthur Kellermann and associates at the Center for Injury Control at Emory University.

Kellermann and associates most recently published studies purported to have found that persons who keep guns in their home, are more likely to be victims of homicide than those who don't. Kellermann's 1986 claim that a gun owner is 43 times more likely to kill a family member than an intruder,[1] the "43 times" fallacy, had been downgraded to the "2.7 times" fallacy by 1993.[2]

In the *Journal of the Medical Association of Georgia*, both Professor Kleck and Dr. Suter found several flaws in Dr. Kellermann's methodology and conclusions. For example, Kellermann's study did not distinguish what percentage of gun uses were for self-protection and which ones were criminal.[3] Moreover, only gun uses that resulted in death were analyzed, thus the study excluded the vast majority of gun uses that do not result in death, and which are more likely to be defensive uses by victims of crime to protect themselves.[3]

Moreover, we now know that the defensive uses of firearms by citizens amount to 2-2.5 million uses per year and dwarf the offensive gun uses by criminals.[4] Between 25-75 lives are saved by a gun for every life lost to a gun.[3] Medical costs saved by guns in the hands of law-abiding citizens are 15 times greater than costs incurred by criminal uses of firearms.[5] Potential victims, with guns to protect themselves, and who know how to use them, are not only more likely to thwart a criminal attack but are also only half as likely to be injured in the process.[6]

As a neurosurgeon familiar with the twin issues of domestic violence and street crime, I also deplore the rising violence and crime in America—but we must have the moral courage to search for the truth and recognize the fact that there is another side to the story that is seldom promulgated. Physicians have a professional obligation to base their opinions on objective data and scientific information rather than on emotionalism or political expediency. And in this light, relevant experience as well as available objective data points out that indiscriminate gun control disarms the law-abiding citizens while it does not prevent criminals and street thugs from perpetrating crimes on unwary victims.

Sadly, public health in general and the Centers for Disease Control and Prevention (CDC) in particular have become grossly politicized, losing sight of their mission and traditional roles of promoting public health and stamping out disease. It has become crystal clear that rather than fulfilling its traditional role, public health has increasingly become a political forum for individuals who consistently advocate politicized health care policies, to the detriment of traditional public health and to the chagrin of many American physicians.

Yes, it is sad that public health, one of the great medical innovations in the age-old, but still ongoing struggle of man against disease, has succumbed to ideology, forfeiting its quest for truth and objectivity in health promotion.

In the name of violence prevention, public health has incessantly promoted a gun control agenda, based not on objective data and quality research, but on flawed data and politicized, result-oriented research at taxpayers' expense, to aid and abet the agenda of those in government who seek to disarm law-abiding citizens using junk science as a vehicle, even and despite, the contrary evidence collected by the criminologic and sociologic literature and the formidable (legal) impediments posed by the Second Amendment.

To this editor—after researching and reviewing this subject critically—it has become obvious that the gun control lobby means to disarm the law-abiding citizen, step-by-step; and they have already gone too far. The crime bill must be reconsidered, and those aspects of it that violate the Second Amendment must be repealed.

There is a crisis of conscience in our society. There is a trend to absolve the individual of personal responsibility and blame society for every illness and affliction. What we need is more individual responsibility and moral accountability, and a tougher criminal justice system without revolving prison doors to reduce domestic violence and street crime in America. And, yes, we need to foster principles of moral and spiritual guidance and family cohesiveness.

As physicians we should not lose our compassion. Yet, when it comes to publishing ground-breaking research and scientific articles, we need to abide by scientific methodology rather than emotionalism and sensationalism. The scientific and epidemiologic data, in fact, support the right of responsible law-abiding individuals "to keep and bear arms" as guaranteed in the Second Amendment to our Constitution.

The Founding Fathers held that man's constitutional rights were God-given and unalienable. Although the government was the guarantor of those rights, it was ultimately on the people themselves that those unalienable rights rested. The informed, vigilant, and armed citizenry were to be the ultimate enforcers, and the Second Amendment itself was to be the vehicle by which this right was to safeguard and secure all others.

The right of law-abiding citizens to keep and bear arms embodied in the Second Amendment must be protected. To preserve our liberty, we must not jump the bandwagon of political expediency or accept junk science and politicized research as the basis for public policy—especially when that policy violates a constitutional right that impairs the ability of law-abiding citizens to protect themselves and defend their families, leaving them at the mercy of criminals who will continue to disobey the law and carry guns illegally.

### REFERENCES

1. Kellermann AL, Reay DT. Protection or peril? An analysis of firearms-related deaths in the home. N Engl J Med 1986;314:1557-1560.
2. Kellermann AL, Rivera FP, Rushforth NB, et al. Gun ownership as a risk factor for homicide in the home. N Engl J Med 1993;329(15):1084-1091.
3. Suter EA. Guns in the medical literature—a failure of peer-review. J Med Assoc Ga 1994;83(13):133-148.
4. Kleck G. Guns and self-protection. J Med Assoc Ga 1994;83(1):42.
5. Suter EA, Waters WC IV, Murray GB, et al. Violence in America—effective solutions. J Med Assoc Ga 1995;84(6):253-263.
6. Gottlieb AM. Gun Rights Fact Book, 1988.

(JUNE, 1995)

CHAPTER 16

# IN SEARCH OF THE FOUNTAIN OF YOUTH

*I don't want to achieve immortality through my work. I want to achieve immortality through not dying.*
Woody Allen

In the aftermath of the conservative revolution of November 8th, we can again ponder some politically incorrect ideas. *Voilà*, instead of "proper allocation of finite and scarce resources," we can indulge to think about longevity, prolonging the lifespan and the quality of life of patients. We can recount the story of medical advances that brought about the unprecedented increase in longevity, particularly in the wake of the Industrial Revolution.

Allow me, then, the indulgence of prefacing my story with the historic tale of the indomitable, Spanish conquistador Juan Ponce de León (c.1460-1521) who discovered and explored Florida in 1513. According to a legend told to him by the natives, there was an elusive "fountain of youth" said to be hidden in the lush vegetation and swampy marshes of the exotic peninsula. In pursuit of this fountain, he went on a fruitless quest. Assailed by hostile Indians, tired, and unsuccessful in his attempts to locate the precious secret, he returned to Cuba. On a return trip in 1521, Ponce de León was, unfortunately, mortally wounded by bellicose Indians near Tampa Bay...before he had found the legendary fountain and been given the opportunity to unravel the secret to man's immortality.

Today, the mythic concept of the "fountain of youth" is perhaps embodied in the dramatic advances made toward the prolongation of lifespan concomitant with gains made in the area of preservation of quality of life. As a result of these advances, octogenarians have become the fastest growing segment of our population in the closing decade of this millennium. Medicine in the 20th Century has performed miraculously in this area, but due to trendy ideologies inherent in the health care debate of the last 2 to 3 years, the significance of these medical advances has taken a back seat to such locutions as the already noted, "proper allocation of

finite and scarce resources," "useful lifespan," "meaningful dialogue...on the right to die,""assisted suicide," etc.

It is time we revisit the pertinent topic of medical advances
and increased longevity, and reincorporate these concepts, as
historic background, for the health care debate that will continue
into the 21st Century, as the aging baby boomers swell the ranks of
the elderly.

## HISTORIC TRENDS

Throughout the Middle Ages, the average human life
expectancy was approximately 7-8 years of age, not only because of
the extremely high perinatal mortality that skewed the data, but also
because Europeans (and much of the world during this time) lived
in an unhealthy milieu of filth, poor hygiene, and nearly non-existent
sanitation. Superstition and ignorance, along with pestilential
diseases and vermin infestation, were rampant. Epidemic and
endemic diseases such as the bubonic plague, typhus, variola, and
the White Death (consumption) took a heavy toll on the population.

In the mid- to late 19th Century, advances brought about by
the Industrial Revolution (c.1750-1850), the germ theory of disease,
public health measures, and the discovery of general anesthesia
culminated in the rise of the scientific era of medicine. The heroes
and heroines of this age included such notable medical figures as:
Edward Jenner (1749-1823), Oliver Wendell Holmes (1809-1894),
Ignaz Semmelweiss (1818-1865), Florence Nightingale (1820-1910),
Rudolf Virchow (1821-1902), Clara Barton (1821-1912), Louis
Pasteur (1822-1895), Joseph Lister (1827-1912), J. Henri Dunant
(1828-1910), Robert Koch (1843-1910)...and many others.

From 1900 to 1930, owing to breakthroughs in the
burgeoning sciences of bacteriology, microbiology, immunology, and
public health—life expectancy was pushed from 47.3 to 59.7 years.
This was an amazing prolongation in life amounting to 12.4 years in
just a generation.[1]

In the 1930s and 1940s, with the introduction of antibiotics
and their widespread use in the post-World War II period, another
great stride was made in the saga of human survival. And it is this
period, corresponding to the widespread usage of antibiotics, that

correlates with today's observed increased longevity.

We should thank the pharmaceutical industry, public health, and, of course, physicians for the progress observed during this period. As you might remember from medical history, puerperal fever was one of those diseases that intrigued and baffled doctors in the 19th Century. You might even remember the famous painting of the illustrious Dr. Oliver Wendell Holmes delivering his famed lecture on the subject to the Boston Medical Society, which, I believe, took place in 1843.

## MATERNAL MORTALITY AND ANTIBIOTICS

Until the arrival of the miracle drug penicillin in the 1940s, the sulfa drugs were the mainstay of antibiotic treatment against infectious diseases. As a result of the availability of sulfa drugs and penicillin, and their widespread use atop earlier public health measures—such as isolation of the sick during epidemics; quarantining of ships at ports of disembarkation; disinfection of fomites; promotion of personal hygiene; furthering of education as to communal sanitation, including the use of potable, running water and the proper disposal of wastes; exposure to fresh air and the beneficial rays of sunlight—life was prolonged beyond all expectations.

Maternal mortality, a dreaded and common complication of pregnancy throughout the ages, was virtually conquered in the 20th Century by the three-prong attack of public health, improved obstetrical care, and the use of antibiotics. The marked reduction in maternal death was indeed one of the great human achievements of medical history. As Drs. N. Hiatt and J.R. Hiatt recently wrote in *The Pharos*: "Maternal mortality was halved every ten years since the introduction of antibiotics in the mid-1930s and now stands below .01%."[1]

Yet, in two of the most salient ironies of recent medical history, in today's litigious climate, obstetricians, who were (and remain) instrumental in improving the maternal morbidity and mortality statistics, are under heavy attack from attorney-litigators in a medical liability crisis which is out of control. Seventy-five percent of U.S. obstetricians have been sued, and young obstetricians are told they should expect to be sued several times during their careers.[2]

For its part, the pharmaceutical industry is also under heavy fire from government bureaucrats for the audacity of remaining in the black during the recessionary period of the last several years. Many other American industries, meanwhile, were submerged in oceans of red ink and asked for subsidies and/or other forms of government protection ("corporate welfare") to survive the "bad times."

Public health has not been exempted either. Recently, it, too, has been increasingly subjected to government propaganda and the prevailing winds of political expediency, as has been the case of AIDS. The dreaded disease caused by the HIV virus has been politicized and treated more as a sociopolitical issue than as the public health menace that it has been (and continues to be) in some sectors of the population.

But let us return to our story and state that the reduction in maternal mortality as well as perinatal infant mortality were to a significant degree responsible for the tremendous rise in life expectancy between 1930 and 1987. Moreover, it was during this time that we conquered such diseases and scourges of humanity as syphilis, pneumonia, diphtheria, typhoid fever, typhus, and the old consumptive killer, tuberculosis—which dropped from the top of the list to #21 in the morbidity and mortality statistics during this time. As a result, life expectancy climbed from 59.7 years in 1930 to 74.9 years by 1987.[1]

Between 1960 and 1987, the average lifespan increased by 5.2 years. Although this climb was not as dramatic as the previous two 30-year increases, it was still a significant improvement.[1] In any event, as we may be approaching our physiologic limits of longevity, lifespan would be expected to increase at a slower pace. Yet, I deeply believe we can still stretch our lifespans considerably while preserving quality of life.

## HAS THE FOUNTAIN BEEN FOUND?

Consider the fact that over 80% of diseases are associated with unhealthy lifestyles and self-destructive behaviors, and thus, they are subject to healthy alterations in behavior.[3,4] The possibilities for improvement are enormous—and maximal lifespan, incidentally, redolent of the search for the secret of the fountain of youth of Ponce de León, has been estimated to be 114 years.[1] A lot of room, then, is still available for improvement!

How, you ask, can we even begin to approach this longevity while remaining fit? Perhaps, by fostering a sense of individual responsibility in our patients; by encouraging them to cease smoking, exercise regularly, stick to proper diets, obtain and remain near ideal body weight, and follow other simple measures which we know can prolong quality time on this resilient Earth. We can even reduce health care costs in the process and save money for when we reach that ripe old, antediluvian age.

Two more items: We need to militate for a revitalized private sector health care system that emphasizes true science and research and development in the medical marketplace, while rewarding those individuals who maintain healthy lifestyles. We need to encourage the pharmaceutical industry to continue to procure new life-saving drugs. And, we also need to derail the litigation juggernaut that is presently devastating both.

### REFERENCES

1. Hiatt N, and Hiatt JR. A history of life expectancy in two developed countries. The Pharos 1992;Spring:2-60.
2. Faria MA Jr. The litigation juggernaut. Part I: The dimensions of the devastation. J Med Assoc Ga 1993;82(8):393-398, and Part II: Strategies and tactics for victory. J Med Assoc Ga 1993;82(9):447-451.
3. Norbeck TB. Telling the truth about rising health care costs. Private Practice 1990;22(2).
4. McGinnis JM, and Foege WH. Actual causes of death in the US. JAMA 1993;270:2207-2212.

(FEBRUARY, 1995)

# CHAPTER 17

# *EPIDEMIC DISEASES AND PUBLIC HEALTH*

*And I looked, and behold, a pale horse; and his name that sat on him was Death.*

Revelation 6:8

*At the peak of his reign in A.D. 540, after accomplishing major political, judicial, and military successes, Justinian's empire was struck by the old enemy of mankind, one that not even Justinian could conquer: pestilential disease. The bubonic plague, which struck with a vengeance in A.D. 540, is justifiably the worst recorded pandemic to ever afflict humanity. Records regarding the dimensions of the devastation, suffering, and death were carefully kept by Justinian's chief archivist, secretary and historian, Procopius....*

*At the time the horrible plague struck, Justinian was engaged in a war that was being waged fiercely on two fronts. We have already described the military feats of his armies as they battled the remnants of the Germanic tribes in the West. But during the years A.D. 541 and 542, Justinian was also engaged in the East fighting the recalcitrant Parthians....*

*If we think of the dimensions of the devastation of the bubonic plague of the 6th Century in the midst of the Dark Ages—the savage imperial wars waged against the barbarian hordes, the terrible famines, the ubiquity of death and destruction, and finally, the full unleashing of the cataclysmic pandemic, the worst pestilence the world has ever seen— it should not be difficult to find within man's psyche invocations against the full horror and conjurations in the face of the surrealistic visitations of the dreaded Four Horsemen of the Apocalypse....*

*Justinian, defeated by the cataclysm, realized that the bubonic plague was a new and unconquerable enemy, an enemy that was demolishing his once invincible armies and killing his generals faster than the wounds inflicted on the battlefield by his mortal enemies. Demoralized and disheartened, he returned to his capital, Constantinople, only to find that there too the terrifying pestilence was relentlessly killing his people, rich and poor, regardless of kinship or station in life.*

*The mortality in the city at this time was approaching 5,000 deaths a day and would eventually reach an all-time high of 10,000 deaths daily. In despair and in need to fill the void, Justinian sought solitude, and the comfort and solace of religion.*

> Excerpted from "The Reign of Justinian"
> and "The Bubonic Plague of The 6th Century"
> *Vandals At The Gates of Medicine*

### INFECTIOUS DISEASES AND LONGEVITY

In a previous essay, "In Search of the Fountain of Youth," I discussed the great advances brought about in research, development, and medical technology which contributed to the unprecedented increased in lifespan in our 20th Century.[1] In this article, I will expand on this same topic, as it relates to strides made by public health in the conquest of infectious diseases and prolongation in lifespan. Here is the story:

Prolongation of productive lifespan took place in the late 19th and early 20th Centuries as a result of the successful conquest of innumerable diseases that had been ravaging mankind since time immemorial. For example, typhoid fever, typhus, and diphtheria (as well as sundry afflictions such as streptococcal and other garden variety bacterial infections that cause pneumonia, gastrointestinal disorders and other ailments) were controlled by a variety of medical and public health measures. Dr. John B. Thomison, Editor Emeritus of the *Southern Medical Journal*, reminds us that, as late as 1898 during the Spanish-American War, America "lost more men to typhoid fever than were killed in battle." And indeed, among U.S. forces (consisting of 107,000 troops), the death toll from typhoid fever was 15,000 deaths out of the 27,000 cases afflicted with the infestation.[2]

As we shall see, the same was true for typhus in World War I. Cleanliness and the much maligned pesticide, DDT, conquered typhus; so that by the time of World War II, typhus had been eradicated and death from this virulent infection was nonexistent.

Childhood diseases, such as whooping cough and measles, and sexually transmitted diseases (STDs), such as syphilis and gonorrhea, and the dreaded disease, tuberculosis, were eventually controlled through improved public health measures, hygiene and sanitation, advancing medical care, and subsequently, the widespread use of antibiotics.

One of the achievements of this era (and it cannot be overstated) was public health's implementation of public education, particularly the need for personal hygiene and public sanitation. In a recent publication, Drs. Nathan and Jonathan R. Hiatt point out that between 1843 and 1858 life expectancy in the U.S. and Great Britain was less than 42 years. With the efforts of Dr. John Snow, a public health advocate and early anesthesiologist who had a keen interest in epidemiology and other issues in public health—such as the use of uncontaminated potable water for drinking and proper disposal of sewage—public health essentially eliminated cholera in Britain by the 1870s and helped stretch the lifespan of British citizens.

The advent of the Industrial Revolution (c.1750-1850) brought an "improved standard of living, higher wages, improved nutrition, cheap soap, and inexpensive cotton clothing" which also contributed to better health and longevity. The typhus epidemics, for instance, were better controlled because cotton clothing, unlike lice-infected woolen, could be washed and rendered free of lice.[3]

The discovery of the germ theory of disease concomitant with the advances in bacteriology and microbiology, the development of antiseptic techniques, and the progressive elimination of dirt and filth, were all major building blocks on which the solid basis for public health, sanitation, and personal hygiene were founded.

All of these measures, taken during the age of scientific medicine in the mid- to late 19th and early 20th Centuries, contributed significantly to the prolongation of life. By 1900, improved nutrition, superior sanitation, and the advances in the field of bacteriology had increased life expectancy to age 47.3.

### THE TUBERCULOSIS BREAKTHROUGH

Before the advent of scientific medicine, tuberculosis was a devastating disease. In the 19th Century, in fact, tuberculosis struck with a vengeance. It was said that when Emperor Napoleon was pursuing his conquest of Europe, fully a quarter of the continent's graves were filled with tuberculosis victims.[4]

Tuberculosis was christened the "White Death" because the skin of those afflicted turned alabaster, thin, and translucent, making small veins visible. Tuberculosis was also called Consumption because it "consumed" the health, strength, and constitution of its victims.[4]

The increase of tuberculosis (also referred to as TB, Tbc, etc.) in the 19th Century, it must be conceded, was due to some aspects of the Industrial Revolution, such as the movement of large numbers of people from rural areas into crowded cities and heavily populated areas.

Tuberculosis was non-discriminatory, for in the end, the White Death took both the poor and the rich, the destitute and the affluent, the masses and the intellectuals. The 19th Century British novelist, Anthony Trollope (1815-1882), succumbed to it, as did his brother and sister, as well as four of his children. Other untimely victims were the Brontë sisters: Emily (1818-1848), Anne (1820-1849), and Charlotte (1816-1855), all of whom died of phthisis, yet another name for this dreaded disease.

The American transcendentalist author of *Walden*, Henry David Thoreau (1817-1862), and the famous Franco-Polish composer and pianist, Frédéric Chopin (1810-1849), also perished from the White Death. So did the English physician, John Keats (1795-1821), who gave up surgery for romantic poetry. Franz Kafka (1883-1924), the Czechoslovakian existentialist philosopher and short story writer, succumbed to TB in the prime of his life. In fact, Panati points out that, in the year Kafka died (1924), over 200,000 Americans also died from tuberculosis.[4]

In 1900, tuberculosis was the third most frequent cause of death with a mortality of 194.4/100,000 population; by 1930, tuberculosis had dropped to fourth, and its mortality had further declined to 71.1/100,000.[5] The improvement was due to better understanding of tuberculosis and its milieu, so that better education could be implemented and sanatoria (isolation) could be instituted; x-ray could be used for diagnosis and follow-up care; improvement could, perhaps, even have resulted from the rudimentary and crude medical treatment of the time: pneumothorax (1898) and thoracoplasty (1911). As a result of these measures, and most importantly, the use of antimicrobial therapy, by 1988, tuberculosis mortality had dropped to the bottom of the list and ranked 21st.

I am in accord with Drs. N. Hiatt and J. R. Hiatt that "the

decline in tuberculosis mortality is only one example of the accomplishments that increased longevity before the age of antibiotics and of modern scientific medicine."[3]

## AIDS AND PUBLIC POLICY

In comparison to the scourge of our age, AIDS, the difference in numbers is astronomical. Despite the publicity rendered to our politicized malady (AIDS), the total number of victims of this new affliction has topped 200,000 in the U.S., a high number, no doubt, but it has taken over a decade to reach this number. By comparison, tuberculosis claimed 200,000 lives in a single year, and then continued to ravage the land year after year, in a United States with a much smaller population pool. Moreover, we know a lot more about AIDS today, than physicians knew about tuberculosis a century ago. In the fight against tuberculosis, public health and physicians worked together with a unified purpose of eradicating the public menace. In contrast, AIDS, a politically protected disease, has been treated as a socio-political issue rather than a public health issue.

Because of the politicization of this disease, medicine's fight against AIDS has become extremely difficult. Physicians and public health officials are not free to fight this epidemic as forcefully as they had been able to do with other diseases in the past. Public health workers and private physicians are still fighting this epidemic with one hand tied behind their backs. The mainstays of public health measures are not utilized because, when it comes to AIDS, physicians are restricted in what they can normally do to contain this dreaded disease. There is no universal testing because of legal restrictions and cumbersome rules regarding counselling, and no contact tracing because confidentiality must be protected at all cost, even if infected individuals place others at risk. Thus, measures to combat AIDS are limited, not only because of circumscriptions in our medical knowledge and the ingenuity and resilience of the virus, but by the force of law and the political expediency of the moment.[6,7]

## PUBLIC HEALTH WOES

Let me conclude by stating that recently the mood of public

health officials was characterized as "somber," as a result of the Republican conservative tsunami that swept Congress and the nation on November 8, 1994.[8]

And, yes, public health advocates do have legitimate reasons for their "somber mood," but not for their "gloomy predictions." It appears that the direction of the new Congress is to refocus public health from an increasingly politicized agency to its former traditional role and more mundane goals of stamping out truly epidimiologic diseases. As a staunch supporter of public health in its former role, I hope public health will heed the message and thereby resume its glorious mission of fighting true pestilential diseases and afflictions, whose culprits truly follow Koch's simple Postulates of Pathogenicity, rather than the trendy ideologies (i.e., politization of AIDs policy and promotion of gun control "research") that have so recently defocused its mission.

### REFERENCES

1. Faria MA Jr. In search of the fountain of youth. J Med Assoc Ga 1995;83:61-62.
2. Thomison JB. On no tracking it around. South Med J 1991;84(7):815-816.
3. Hiatt N, and Hiatt JR. A history of life expectancy in two developed countries. The Pharos 1992;Spring:52-60.
4. Panati C. Extraordinary Endings of Practically Everything and Everybody. New York, Harper and Row Publishers, 1989.
5. Historical statistics of the U.S.: Colonial times to 1970. Bicentennial edition, Washington, D.C., U.S. Dept. of Commerce. Bureau of the Census, 1975. Cited in Hiatt and Hiatt, op. cit.
6. Faria MA Jr. To treat or not to treat—can a physician choose? The Pharos 1992;55(1):39-40.
7. Fumento M. The Myth of Heterosexual AIDS. New York, Basic Books Publishers, 1990.
8. Faria MA Jr. Public health has reasons to fear the new Congress. Am Med News, January 1995.

(MAY, 1995)

# CHAPTER 18

# *AIDS AND MEDICAL CORRECTNESS*

Many Americans, even physicians, are unaware that the National Research Council, which is an arm of the National Academy of Sciences, proclaimed in February 1993 that "the AIDS epidemic will have little impact on the lives of most Americans or the way society functions." Moreover, the CDC has released the year-end AIDS figures for 1992 which show that "the overall cases increased only 3.5% from the year before, less than the 5% increase from 1990-1991." Furthermore, as recently reported by *National Review*, the CDC enunciated that it was revising downward its estimate of future AIDS cases; it seems, therefore, that Michael Fumento's book, *The Myth of Heterosexual AIDS*, will be vindicated after all.

Nevertheless, the AIDS activists have had enough muscle to coerce the CDC to broaden the description of AIDS to avert the flattening of the curve of the AIDS epidemic. This tactic would, of course, again balloon the number of AIDS victims and create the illusion that we are all still vulnerable, so as to preserve the momentum of a pandemic, and thereby, achieve the goals of their narrow political agenda: Retain their supremacy of government medical (research and prevention) dollars and attain not just acceptance of the gay and lesbian lifestyle, but also approval and bestowal of special group rights.

As if to underscore this objective, HHS Secretary Donna Shalala—who has no medical credentials but did obtain the reputation as the "Priestess of Political Correctness," a reputation gained as a former Chancellor at the University of Wisconsin—has entered the fray. In response to a question about welfare reform, she told a Congressional panel: "We could spend our energy on research and immunization and education and still not have any Americans left unless we're prepared to confront the crisis of AIDS."

I would like to point out one of the most salient of the inequities (and iniquities) inherent to the politics of AIDS, which unfortunately, has become entrenched in today's political establishment, and that is, the allocation, or rather, the misallocation of health care resources.

As far back as 1991, the Congressional Research Service of the Library of Congress showed the disproportionate amount of research and prevention funds allocated to AIDS in comparison to other maladies associated with much greater morbidity and death rates. Here are the statistics (1990):

| DISEASE | RESEARCH AND PREVENTION | DEATHS |
|---|---|---|
| Cancer | $1,810,000,000 | 518,000 |
| Heart Disease | $ 708,000,000 | 716,000 |
| Diabetes | $ 295,000,000 | 36,000 |
| Alzheimer's | $ 243,000,000 | 100,000 |
| AIDS | $1,950,000,000 | 36-45,000 |

And according to even more recent data, we find that for fiscal year 1992, the expenditure for AIDS's research and development again tops the list and is in excess of $3.5 billion dollars. Meanwhile, breast cancer with three times the cumulative 10-year mortality as that of AIDS (Breast Cancer: 450,000 deaths *vis-à-vis* AIDS: 150,000 deaths) is funded for a fraction of that allocated to AIDS—such is the power of a vocal, militant special interest group.

And here are more grim statistics: approximately 175,000 women are diagnosed with breast cancer yearly, while 45,000 die from the disease. Sadly, breast cancer's lifetime risk for American women climbed to 1-in-9 women in 1991 (from 1-in-10 in 1987), and to make a tragedy of an already somber story, breast cancer rates continue to increase slowly, year after year.

While it is true that young women can follow several recommendations—to enhance their chances of survival from breast cancer, e.g., do their utmost to have the diagnosis of breast cancer made early (i.e., perform monthly self-examinations, keep medical appointments, and undergo routine mammography as directed by their physicians), and can themselves reduce the risk simply by being mothers (e.g., having children and avoiding abortions) and breast-feeding their babies—they can do little at present to change their genetic predisposition that comes with their family history. Moreover, since breast cancer rates increase with age, there is no solace in advancing age. Younger women are not exempt from this tragic affliction since young women ages 25 to 45 are vastly represented in the morbidity and mortality figures. Yet, feminist leaders—instead of confronting these grave statistics and fighting for proper funding for breast cancer research—have joined the homosexual lobby, and together, are militating for an ultra-liberal political agenda for society. It is too bad that they are neither inclined nor enthused to push this life and death issue onto the forefront of politics. Proper funding for breast cancer research should have been a goal paramount in their agenda.

On the other hand, in the United States most AIDS victims are male (over 90%), homosexual or bisexual, or intravenous drug abusers of both sexes—accounting for more than 86% of AIDS deaths. In these cases, the truth, although politically and socially incorrect, is that the individuals, to a significant degree, are themselves responsible by their self-destructive behaviors—not just the behavior of male homosexuals and the well known, high rate of promiscuity and multiple unknown partners, but also the dangerous and potentially lethal practice of unprotected anal intercourse.

There are, nevertheless, another 14% or so afflicted with this unforgiving malady, who are completely innocent bystanders. Nevertheless, they all deserve our attention and compassion. Yet, we do have a duty to point out these unsavory facts and matter of life and death statistics, and the need for individual responsibility.

And, as the old adage says, "the squeaky wheel gets the grease"—although in this context, the old adage attains a much more solemn tone, in a very ominous context. But the observation is a fact: the obstreperous, irreverent, and vocal homosexual lobby, e.g., ACT-UP, has taken a disproportionately large piece of the research and development pie, and they will continue to prevail politically, because such is the power of the well-focused, well organized, vociferous, and militant special interest groups, to the detriment of others who remain relatively silent and have no such stridency or political clout.

(OCTOBER, 1993)

# PART FIVE: MANAGED CARE, CORPORATE SOCIALIZED MEDICINE, AND MEDICAL ETHICS

CHAPTER 19

# *MANAGED CARE AND THE RISK OF LITIGATION*

As I began to write this editorial, I must confess I was over-whelmed by the many spin-offs of the managed care/managed competition maelstrom that I felt I needed to cover; yet, I could not settle on one topic. At least three related items seemed to me too important to be omitted from this discussion. I finally settled on managed care litigation. Other issues will become evident in the pages of ensuing chapters. Bear with me as we discuss these important items. Keep in mind that as I write these words, Mrs. Hillary Rodham Clinton and her Health Care Task Force have not yet unveiled their proposals. But by the time you read this, those proposals would have been placed on the table for discussion by the health care pundits and eventual legislation by our elected representatives in Congress.

Health care in general and managed care in particular are hot items in the health care economic and political arena, and thus, countless middlemen and intermediaries are flocking to form managed care networks to get their share of the health care pie. One prescription for reform endorsed by some close advisors to the President would establish Health Care Purchasing Cooperatives (HCPCs) to fit the new managed competition paradigm of health care delivery. This new tier of bureaucracy would intercede between health insurers and the buyer—be they individuals or employers. In addition, I suspect, an old industry would be fortified and further entrenched to sap the life of American physicians—the sue-for-profit litigation industry.[1]

At the 1992 MAG Leadership Conference held in Atlanta, I learned an important item from a poignant lecture given by Mr. James W. Cannon, Jr., J.D., a partner in the prestigious Austin, Texas law firm of Akin, Gump, Strauss, Hauer, and Feld. Mr. Cannon, a defense attorney warned about the treat of a looming dagger materializing while aimed at the hearts of physicians enrolling in managed care and managed competition plans.

Mr. Cannon said that Health Maintenance Organizations

(HMOs) were potentially "a burning fire of liability for physicians and hospitals." He expected that as these organizations continued to expand, they would provide fertile ground for medical lawsuits filed against physicians and hospitals for several reasons, but of which one is of paramount importance. According to Mr. Cannon, this one paramount reason is based on the fact that the *raison d'être* for HMOs is to restrict care and contain costs. It is common knowledge that in general HMO primary care physicians, while intended to be used as gatekeepers to restrict access to specialists, are also under immense pressure to see as many patients as possible, as to make the HMO more efficient and profitable.

The problem with this set up is that courts and juries in medical liability cases see it differently. As juries see it, according to Mr. Cannon, patients see physicians to receive care, and, I might add, expecting physicians to abide by the ethical principle of putting patients, not costs, first. In point of fact, while the public decries the high cost of medical care, when in the jury box, they see it differently. Expenses are not seen as a factor which should impede physicians from doing all they can for their patients.

And since in hindsight everyone has 20/20 vision, the physicians will be judged on what they failed to do for their patients—acts of omission. The plaintiff's attorney is not only going to point out this alleged omission, but will also link it to the fact that the physician was an HMO physician who had voluntarily entered into a contractual agreement with an entity whose fundamental reason for existence is not better patient care, but cost containment. Mr. Cannon cited one illustrative case in which a hospital was encumbered with a $52 million verdict.

In fact, this issue of potential substandard care, or alleged substandard care, attributed to managed care schemes in association with medical malpractice has come to the attention of physicians familiar with managed care. On March 13, 1993, *The Macon Telegraph* reported that in one of the meetings on health care delivery held by the First Lady, this exact point was brought up by a physician from Tampa, Florida. In that particular 6-hour session, Dr. Cornelius I.C. Turabalba, a radiation oncologist from Bradenton, cautioned "against pushing Americans into health maintenance organizations." He then added that, HMOs had pressured him "to take care of patients in a 'substandard way.' "

Moreover, *Physician's Weekly* on January 20, 1992, reported rife dissatisfaction at the Harvard Community Health Plan, "one of the nation's model HMOs." The salaried doctors at that HMO "mutinied" because of plans to tie 15% of their pay to productivity quotas and the administration's demand that primary care physician's "average 15-minutes a patient."

With managed care/managed competition, the bottom line is cost containment not quality of care, and therefore physicians must be ever vigilant of their patients' welfare. It should also be noted that given the fact that taxation of health benefits is one of the pillars of managed competition, and the new envisioned tax structure would favor HMO entities, managed competition experts favor direct federal encouragement of HMOs in one fashion or another.* Managed care and managed competition then are inextricably interwoven and for the purpose of this editorial, they are being discussed together.

All of this, coupled with the fact that tort reform does not appear to be a priority in this administration, is as unfortunate as it is disheartening for American physicians. We can expect no respite from medicolegal litigation. As things now stand, more likely the opposite will be the case, especially if we proceed with managed care and/or managed competition and no tort reform is instituted.

### LITIGATION-ON-DEMAND

For physicians, health care reform resulting in either managed care or managed competition without tort reform, to control litigation-on-demand, is a tinder box waiting for a spark to ignite it whenever a dissatisfied patient does not obtain the desired medical result.

Unless physicians mobilize soon, we can expect the First Lady, her advocate-advisor friends at the Children's Defense Fund (CDF), and the Trial Lawyers Association, to push for litigation to

---

* It has become apparent HMOs are favored by federal policy, not only through the tax structure (i.e., The HMO Act of 1975), but also with antitrust exemption and immunity from medical liability (i.e., the McCarran-Ferguson Act and ERISA [Employment Retirement Income Security Act] statutes).

continue unrestricted with the goal of exorcising all of the perceived evils of American society and capitalism, including the omnipresent alleged health care transgressors. We must not lose sight of the fact that liberal plaintiff's attorneys view the sue-for-profit litigation industry in which they avidly participate, not for what it really is, but as a moral crusade undertaken both for righting societal wrongs and for correcting what they perceive as the maldistribution of wealth in American society.

Nor do I need to remind you of at least two memoranda that became public during the Presidential campaign closely associating the then-Presidential candidate and his friends in the Arkansas Trial Lawyers Association. The memoranda intimated that Mr. Clinton had no inclination of pushing for any meaningful tort reform package if he became President. Furthermore, since that time, he has stated that for reduction of medical litigation, he will rely primarily on *practice parameters*—which, the story goes, if a physician follows, he will be presumed to have not committed malpractice. But, as everyone familiar with legal jargon knows, that presumption can be easily overcome by a simple accusation or the filing of a lawsuit with an "expert" affidavit which is, anyway, required in most states. His other suggestion, *Alternative Dispute Resolution (ADR)*, is more imbued in rhetoric than in substance, as it is suspected that it will not consist of effective *Pre-trial Screening Panels or binding arbitration*. The former would have reviewed a complaint before a lawsuit could be filed to weed out those that were frivolous; the latter, would have bypassed the civil court trial system.

Instead, Clinton's ADR will consist of a watered down *non-binding mediation* board which would render a particular opinion in a case, that may or may not influence the jurors at the time of trial. Since it is non-binding, it would not stop lawsuits from being filed or prevent the physician from going through the imposition of years of a lawsuit nightmare.

As I have said before, the time is now for physicians to be involved in organized medicine and health care issues. They must join the organization that reflects their views, ethics, and is willing to fight for their interests. By the same token, physicians must cease to blindly assume or hope that the leadership of those organizations will "do the right thing." Physicians must be actively involved and must remember that they have a legal obligation to abide by an organization's bylaws and ethical pronouncements.[2]

It is imperative that physicians not only understand all the ramifications of managed care/managed competition, including potential liability, but also recognize the need for active involvement in organized medicine. Physicians need to make sure that the organization that represents them is not just giving lip service to political expediency, but is representing their interests and those of their patients, as well as those of the profession at large. Otherwise, medical practitioners, like the serfs of medieval Europe, will find themselves one day bound by the yoke of an omnipotent government—members of an enslaved profession relegated to involuntary servitude for ages to come.

### REFERENCES

1. Olson WK. The Litigation Explosion—What Happened When America Unleashed the Lawsuit. Truman Talley Books, Dutton, New York, 1991.
2. Berg RN. The ethical practice of medicine. J Med Assoc Ga 1990;79(11):863-864.

(JUNE, 1993)

## CHAPTER 20

# *SLEEPING WITH THE ENEMY*

As you may or may not know, there are no physicians from organized medicine serving on Mrs. Clinton's Health Care Task Force—MDs who represent practitioners and their patients. Those MDs who are on the task force, according to the AMA, are mostly "federal employees" who do not represent the profession. It is reasonable to assume that more likely they represent the bureaucracies whence they came and which sign their paychecks.

A few years ago, I believe it was at the time of his ascension to the top of the AMA totemic hierarchy, Dr. James S. Todd, Executive Vice-President of the AMA, announced quite ceremoniously we had entered a "new era of cooperation, not confrontation." And indeed, a new era began. But, it has not been an era of mutual cooperation, as we were led to believe, in which government and medicine entered a new phase of cooperation for the mutual benefit of the medical profession and their patients on the one hand, and the government policymakers and bureaucrats on the other. Instead of cooperation, we have been ushered down a one-way street of progressive government intrusion into the practice of medicine, facilitated by the AMA serving as the vehicle inducing passivity and submission in our ranks. The AMA, in the view of many physicians, has served not to represent the interest of physicians and their patients, but instead to assume, willingly at worse or unwittingly at best, the role of a collaborator. And, as collaborator, has only softened the hard blows that have repeatedly befallen the medical profession. By making these otherwise mortal blows just barely tolerable, physicians have acquiesced to the terrible calamities that have befallen their profession; and thus, the unholy alliance has successfully prevented open rebellion in the physicians' ranks. Up to this time, the government authorities and their bureaucratic machine, oiled by the so-called health care experts, have succeeded in taking us, as a profession, step-by-step, closer to the government abbatoir of corporate socialized medicine.

I know these are hard words, but I speak so directly

because I sense that the time of reckoning for Medicine is fast approaching, and courage is needed to tell the truth. I speak not to condemn, but with the hope that historical lessons about human nature are learned here for a better future.

Yes, the AMA Board of Trustees all too often has been eager to please our adversaries, like British Prime Minister Neville Chamberlain in 1938, who, having returned to London from the Munich Conference with Hitler and Mussolini, gleefully and with an air of great self-accomplishment exclaimed, "I bring you peace in our time," as he waved the fleeting document that sealed the fate of the world for the next decade with its bloody World War II and thence, the stark beginning of the Cold War with the building of the Berlin Wall and the descension of the Iron Curtain across Europe from the Baltic to the Black Sea.

And more recently, in our own country, let us recall what happened when President George Bush having dissociated himself from his Republican conservative brethren to collaborate with his unyielding rivals, the liberal Democratic congressional leadership, forged the disastrous Budget Reconciliation Act of 1990 which raised taxes thereby breaking his "read my lips, no new taxes" pledge. Yet, Congress did not keep its side of the bargain, cutting spending, and fell back to its old ways, tax and tax and spend again. The result was a protracted and painful recession, further escalation of the national debt, and ultimately, his own repudiation as President by the American electorate and the consequent election of President Bill Clinton last November.

So, I was not in the least surprised as I skimmed through the morning paper and read, "President Clinton Thursday rebuffed the nations largest medical organization [AMA] calling it a special interest group that doesn't belong on his health care task force.... 'You cannot get anything done if special interest groups sit in on those meetings...' "[1]

It is therefore no wonder that despite the highly politicized times in which we live, in which ever-increasing numbers of individuals are flocking to join every conceivable special interest group to protect their own self-interest, the AMA represents barely 40% of the nation's 718,000 physicians. And, within the medical profession, physicians are disunited, fragmented into a myriad of organizations pushing and pulling in opposite directions—a situation which has made us easy prey for our adversary-predators. Thus, these predators did not even have to divide us, they only had to conquer us!

To add insult to injury, Representative Fortney "Pete" Stark (D-CA), charged, "the AMA is trying to take control of the health care reform....Basically, the AMA would like to be the principal negotiating agent, the big muckety-muck. That is not going to happen." "Pete" Stark, it should be noted, ranked No. 1 in political contributions, collecting $497,250 for the decade ending June 30, 1991. Common Cause reports that of that amount, he amassed $203,200 from medical political action committees (PACs), placing him in the No.2 position in contributions from our own ranks.

The AMA, which had called for a new era of "cooperation and non-confrontation" with the government, and more recently, "a new partnership," was slapped in the face and scoffed publicly. In fact, when I read about it in the newspaper, I felt like Winston Churchill, who, describing the Munich Conference of 1938 between English Prime Minister Neville Chamberlain and the dictators, Hitler and Mussolini, decried, "We have sustained a defeat without a war" (House of Commons, October 5, 1938).

Appeasement does not stop tyranny. It nurtures despotism. Yet, our leadership has been inclined to appease and to coax our enemies, government bureaucrats and self-styled consumer advocates (who lately, also profess to be health care experts), rather than to fight them with the truth, much to the detriment of the medical profession. Largely to blame has been the direction of the AMA in recent years as dictated by its powerful leadership: the Board of Trustees and the Council on Ethical and Judicial Affairs. This sorry state of affairs in the practice of medicine has been to a significant degree the result of the AMA leaders placing imagery over substance, displaying a lack of vision, and a lack of moral courage to stand by those whom they represent, while possessing a misguided belief that it's below their dignity to roll up their sleeves and get their hands dirty in the political arena to fight for the rights of their confreres (and their patients) and the interest of the profession.

With the adoption of an appeasement policy by the AMA, it was left to the Association of American Physicians and Surgeons

(AAPS) to file a lawsuit (*AAPS v. Clinton*) to force open the secret meetings of the Health Care Task Force which had been held behind closed doors, and perhaps illegally—that is the contention of the organization led by Jane M. Orient, M.D., Executive Director of the AAPS. The AAPS has already won a legal victory in New Jersey where Dr. Lois Copeland and several of her Medicare patients fought successfully to contract privately for medical services outside Medicare while allowing patients to preserve their Medicare benefits (*Stewart et al. v. Sullivan*).

What is so ironic is, for all the years of collaboration and accommodation of government intrusion, now at the time of near reckoning, the AMA leadership has been scoffed (e.g., not given the much coveted seat at the table and derisively called a special interest), and physicians in general and AMA members in particular have been abandoned to the wolves.

A letter to the editor by Charles L. Hoffman, M.D. of San Rafael, California, in the March issue of *Private Practice* summarizes it very well: "Years ago I wrote to James S. Todd, M.D., Executive Director of the AMA, and suggested that the AMA quit trying to be all things to all people and act like an advocate on behalf of the members who support them. The lay public perceives the AMA as the 'doctor's union,' so why shouldn't the AMA function as such on our behalf? Dr. Todd never answered me."[2]

And the truth is this sorry state of affairs for medicine, including the fact that at this moment we do not have physician representation on the Health Care Task Force, should never have been allowed to happen. For the system to work, it must have input from the highly-trained physicians and compassionate healers who deliver health care.

Unfortunately, it seems the government now takes physicians for granted. It should think twice before prodding us to take the final step. Harry Schwartz, Ph.D., in the same March issue of *Private Practice* has called for the formation of physicians' unions with the power to strike, not as a matter of gaining any favors from government, but as a matter of principle and professional survival.[3]

And to end this admonition, let us recall the words of that great Italian epic poet, Dante Alighieri (1265-1321), who trained as a physician, but is remembered more as a theologian, social critic, and man of letters. He, himself, so admonished: "The hottest places in Hell are reserved for those who, in time of great moral crisis, maintain their neutrality."

### REFERENCES

1. USA Today, March 5, 1993.
2. Hoffman CL. No answer from the AMA. Private Practice 1993;25(3):8.
3. Schwartz H. Up against the wall—are doctors running out of options? Private Practice 1993;25(3):13-16.

(JUNE, 1993)

## CHAPTER 21

# HAMMURABI, DEFENSIVE MEDICINE, AND PRACTICE GUIDELINES

*The world owes all its onward impulses to men ill at ease. The happy man
inevitably confines himself within ancient limits.*
Nathaniel Hawthorne (1804-1864)

### ON MANAGED CARE AND CUTTING-EDGE TECHNOLOGY

In the wake of the epochal November '94 elections that
swept conservatives to power, and hopefully a new philosophy of
health reform—viz, economic incentives to promote healthy
lifestyles and the pursuit of longevity—it is appropriate and relevant
we discuss the new vistas of opportunities for cutting-edge technologies in the biomedical industries and the potential impediments
to health progress.

Despite the presently available medical networks for
communication via Cybermedix and the Information
Superhighway, the greatest impediment to this "state of the art"
technology reaching clinical medicine and patients any time soon,
remains the present atmosphere of cost controls, covert rationing of
medical care, and litigation- (of individual physicians, not the
networks which are shielded) on-demand.

Managed competition—the prevailing philosophy of
health care delivery with its centerpiece, managed care, incarnated
in HMOs—does not have the advancement of cutting-edge
technology, promotion of academic medicine, or the prolongation of
life expectancy as its primary goals, but the implementation of cost
control mechanisms and the fiscal realization of the bottom line, as
the ultimate objectives. We will have more to say later about cost
controls and rationing in the managed care/managed competition
model.

Managed care may be free-market for the health system
network megacorporations, but not for the traditional innovators of
medical technology (the medical scientists and entrepreneurs of
yore), nor for physicians and their patients, who will relate under a

new set of ethics and a yet-to-be-determined "new model" of the patient-doctor relationship.[1]

Unless we are very careful and actively oppose the present trend, the role of gatekeeper will be amplified from that of following practice guidelines (or parameters) and restricting access to specialists and complex treatments, to that of actively denying their patients referral to new and expensive technologies and to potentially life-saving, "experimental" treatments and procedures.

I'm deeply concerned in the present *zeitgeist* and under the prevailing winds of cost controls and persistent interference in the patient-doctor relationship, further restrictions will be made— be that via the denial of coverage of procedures deemed "experimental," or "not appropriate or medically necessary" by utilization review personnel responsive to the cost control incentives of the HMOs that employ them. Also quite disturbing are the reports about the increasing practice of "off-the-cuff" diagnoses (without the benefit of the appropriate diagnostic studies such as MRIs or CT scans until late in the progress of the illness) made by managed care physicians attempting to hold down costs that frequently are proved to be "off-the-mark"; instead, not infrequently, this practice results in damaging and costly lawsuits.[2] (And, in this setting, I will be the first to admit lawsuits would not only be justified, but necessary to protect patients from wayward, unethical "providers.")

It does not take a lot of cogitation and analysis to realize that the relationship of managed care and the implementation of new (and frequently) expensive technologies pose a new problem in health care delivery. As things now stand, characterization of a treatment modality as an "experimental procedure" could result in denial of care, and consequently, more lawsuits and stagnation of medical innovation as well as further erosion of the already strained patient-doctor relationship.

Unless truly free-market principles are put firmly in place in the delivery of medical care, particularly research and development, I suspect we could end up with a scarcity of new medical treatments and procedures, if not frank regression in everyday clinical practice, negating the great medical strides made since the turn of the century

Today, a gatekeeper may be a conscientious "primary care"

physician, or physician's assistant, or even a nurse practitioner. Tomorrow, he may be a savvy medical provider who would undercut his colleagues economic base because of a willingness to apply more flexible ethics and display a disposition that more easily conforms to the wishes of the third-party payers or the government.

And this brings us to the ultimate question: Do we want to continue to extend (or resume our drive towards) improving life expectancy (concomitant with enhancements in quality of life), advance superior and cutting-edge technology, or should we keep the course of today's self-proclaimed health care experts and bio-medical ethicists who believe that overt rationing is inevitable, and thus, we should relent to the present limits of scientific technology? For myself, I will opt for the *patient-oriented, free-market approach** to medical care and for the continued expansion of the vistas of medical knowledge. Those who would chose the latter option, I suppose, will be content to use low-level of care palliation for the chronically ill and those suffering from the ravages of advancing age, while promoting the drive toward the more aggressive use of advanced directives and other right-to-die reforms leading incipiently toward active euthanasia.

And for those who say we can not afford to expand the limits of medical technology much longer because of burgeoning population, and "the proper allocation of finite resources," I say: "Yes we can." Look at the thriving nations of the Pacific Rim in Asia: Taiwan, Singapore, Malaysia, Indonesia, and Hong Kong—all of which, under the banner of free-market capitalism, individual incentives, and the application of advancing technology—are becoming prosperous communities with higher standards of living and with individuals living healthier and longer than their counterparts in India and Africa who continue to languish under the old, discredited ideas of socialism and collectivism.

If we are not quick to learn and make amends about the impediments that managed competition poses to medical advances, research and development, we may find ourselves falling behind in the communication and biomedical, technologic revolutions of the 21st Century.

* See Chapter 4, pp. 37-39.

Perhaps we should look at the lessons of history for guidance and using its wisdom address two pressing problems brought on by new developments in medical care—the implementation of practice guidelines with its concomitant reduction in innovation in medical progress, in general, and medical technology, in particular, and the practice of defensive medicine with its resulting decrease in the quality of medical care.

## HAMMURABI'S MEDICAL LEGACY—DEFENSIVE MEDICINE IN EGYPT c.1750-1500 B.C.

The Code of Hammurabi strictly and harshly dealt with an "eye for an eye" justice, as well as general medical jurisprudence in Akkadian Babylonia, c.1750 B.C. For example, regarding surgical fees and operations, the Code promulgated:

*If a physician shall cause on anyone a severe operation wound with a bronze operating-knife and cure him, or if he shall open a tumor (abscess or cavity) with a bronze operating-knife and save the eye of the patient, he shall have ten shekels of silver; if it is a slave, his owner shall pay two shekels of silver to the physician.*

*If a physician shall make a severe wound with the bronze operating-knife and kill him, or shall open a growth with a bronze operating-knife and destroy the eye, his hands shall be cut off.*

*If a physician shall make a severe wound with a bronze operating-knife on the slave of a freed man and kill him, he shall replace the slave with another slave. If he shall open an abscess (growth, tumor, cavity) with a bronze operating-knife and destroy the eye, he shall pay the half of the value of the slave.*

*If a physician shall heal a broken bone or cure diseased bowels, he shall receive five shekels of silver; if it is a matter of a freed slave, he shall pay three shekels of silver; but if a slave, then the master of the slave shall give to the physician two shekels of silver....*[3]

The Code of Hammurabi profoundly affected medical practice, not just in Babylonia and Mesopotamia but also in faraway lands and empires, such as existed then in ancient Egypt—far more than had ever been imagined. Egyptian physicians were in fact subject to many strict rules and harsh regulations as a result of the pervasive influence of the Code of Hammurabi. This is further corroborated by Dr. James Salander's (Associate Professor of Surgery at Walter Reed Army Medical Center, Bethesda, Maryland) fascinating study of the Edwin Smith Papyrus, considered by some scholars to be the world's oldest surgical textbook. After years of researching a translation of the papyrus (a copy translated and annotated by the renowned scholar James Henry Breasted), Salander was able to elucidate very interesting details regarding medical knowledge and the practice of medicine in Egypt c.1500 B.C.

Salander confirmed that the papyri were a collection of 48 cases, 45 of which were trauma cases. Case stories were presented "in anatomical sequence, beginning with injuries of the head and onward down the body." In the papyri, he continues, "each case is assigned a prognosis...." Then a very important ethical statement follows: "In cases in which an injury was so severe that a favorable outcome seemed unlikely, the practitioner declined to treat the patient. Fifteen of the 45 trauma cases received unfavorable verdicts." The report went on to say, "not all patients denied care suffered devastating injuries." For example, closed fractures of the mandible and open-rib and nasal fractures were all considered "untreatable."[4]

The student of history will agree with Salander's explanation for the unfavorable prognoses rendered in these cases, and that is, that the strong influence of the Code of Hammurabi which "holds strict accountability to the physician with uncomfortably severe penalties...," made Egyptian physicians wary of treating those injuries which carried a high degree of failure or deformity. Thus, rather than treating these common injuries with the medical expertise they were known to possess, they falsely rendered the prognoses unfavorable and abstained from treating those unfortunate patients whose injuries they considered too risky and likely to result in severe or lethal reprisals.

The implications, of course, are tremendous and very relevant to the present adversarial litigious climate that permeates our society. What we have found here is that knowledgeable Egyptian physicians, the most knowledgeable in the ancient world, were advising that medical treatment be withheld as a self-protective measure—*defensive medicine*—against the potential harsh government reprisals applicable in cases of treatment failure in victims with life-threatening wounds, or as in the case of nasal fractures, patient dissatisfaction.

### PRACTICE GUIDELINES AND MEDICAL PROGRESS

Like Moses, who received the Ten Commandments from God, Hammurabi claimed to have received his laws from the Babylonian sun-god, Shamash, god of justice. The laws are inscribed in 4000 lines of Akkadian cuneiform writing containing 300 legal provisions covering not only an oppressive code of medical ethics but also voluminous rules regulating businesses, criminal laws, agricultural provisions, and rules of conduct in all ways of life, public and private.

The jurisdiction of the Code was enforced by the King and his jurists throughout the kingdom and established what became known as "an eye for an eye" justice: The state was supreme. The Code was extremely oppressive to medical practitioners and thus impeded medical innovation. Medical progress would have to flourish elsewhere.

Codified laws were for the first time formulated to regulate public health and enumerate the duties and responsibilities of physician-priests. Along with these duties went stiff legal penalties...thus, as we have seen under King Hammurabi, the first code of "ethics" was imposed on the medical profession.

Many centuries later, in his travels amongst the Babylonians, Herodotus (5th Century B.C.), the Father of History, noted:

*They bring out their sick to the market-place, for they have no physicians; then those who pass by the sick person confer with him about the disease, to discover whether they have themselves been afflicted with the same disease as the sick person, or have seen others so afflicted; thus the passers-by confer with him, and advise him to have recourse to the same treatment as that by which they escaped a similar disease, or as they have known to cure others. And they are not allowed to pass by a sick person in silence, without inquiring into the nature of his distemper....*[5]

What Herodotus had so clearly described is the *regression*

of Babylonian medicine to a primitive state of affairs. Once again, as a result of oppressive government intervention, medical practice (and ethics) had deteriorated. We learn from the writings of Herodotus that, so oppressive had become the state of affairs for practitioners, that physicians had become scarce or non-existent, and thus, the whole community was forced to act as a sort of medical collective, utilizing a communal approach to treat the many illnesses and afflictions suffered by the common folks.

Yet, in Egypt, as is evident by thorough and careful review of the Edwin Smith Papyrus, the physician-priests were known to have definite knowledge about the diagnosis, treatment, and even prognosis of the traumatic injuries, that later physicians were loathe to treat.

In short, knowledgeable Egyptian physicians were forced to withhold certain high-risk surgeries and even relatively innocuous procedures (that is, practice *defensive medicine*) to fend off harsh but lawful reprisals from potentially poor outcomes (*medical liability*).

We can surmise that Mesopotamian (Babylonian) surgery which was even more restricted was hampered even further, with the result that there were no significant innovations, and progress was essentially nil—all as a result of the natal and closer legacy of the harsh Code of Hammurabi.

From the foregoing what is eminently clear is that the practice of medicine cannot thrive in a milieu of government oppression, coercion, and intimidation, and as we have just found, this is true, whether we are speaking of an antediluvian era 4,000 years ago or the worsening, deteriorating practice environment of today.

Let us all hope that health care reform in its present format (managed care/managed competition) is rejected, and the real problems in the American health care system addressed at a more propitious time and in the not-too-distant future—for, in the great scheme of things, we are here to accomplish much, if only for a brief, fleeting, epochal moment.

### REFERENCES

1. Faria MA Jr. Vandals at the Gates of Medicine—Historic Perspectives on the Battle

Over Health Care Reform. Hacienda Publishing, Inc., Macon, Georgia, 1995, pp. 255-263.
2. Salerno S. High price of managed care. The Wall Street Journal, January 18, 1994.
3. Faria, op. cit., p. 25.
4. Ibid., pp. 25-26.
5. Ibid., p. 36.

(MARCH, 1995; A VERSION OF THIS ARTICLE ALSO APPEARED IN THE SUMMER 1996 ISSUE OF THE *MEDICAL SENTINEL*.)

CHAPTER 22

# THE ETHICS OF CORPORATE
# SOCIALIZED MEDICINE

*It is the free mind and individual responsibility, the principles
of the Renaissance which have brought us the wonders of modern health
care through the free-market capitalist system and through the inven-
tiveness of the free minds it has raised. It seems we are now going to
harness the capitalist engine for rationing....*

*It seems that we in America are about to embark on an
accelerated venture of harnessing the capitalist engine for the destruction
of healing....For instance, the terms managed competition we hear in all
these proposals, by sleight of words say the opposite of what they mean.
It is competition in management we should be speaking of....It is the loss
of philosophical concepts, the loss of the spirit of free will and individual
responsibility represented in these schemes, together with conceptual
muddle-headedness which are sounding the death knell to the philosophy
of our civilization.*[1]

Thomas A. Dorman, M.D.

As we further reflect on what transpired during the health
care reform debate of 1993 and 1994, we must realize more than
just changes in the U.S. health care delivery system were (and are
still) at stake. As you would remember, the government launched an
all-out attack to seize control of the American health care industry,
and with it, 15% of the GNP, in one giant scoop. That attack was
successfully repulsed by the American public who rejected the
colossal state bureaucracy inherent to that scheme of socialized
medicine.

But a clear and present danger still looms on the medical
horizon, and that is, *corporate socialized medicine* in the form of
managed care/managed competition. Where once the supreme
medical ethic dictated that physicians place their individual
patients' interest above their own (and above that of the state) in the
spirit of true altruism and charity, today's ethics of corporate
socialized medicine and managed competition propound that the
physician place cost considerations and the interest of third-party
payers above that of his or her patient. That is, they want physicians

to practice what the Swiss philosopher, Professor Ernest Truffer, calls a *veterinary ethic* which rejects the traditional medical ethic requiring a physician to care for his/her patient according to the patient's specific medical requirements, in favor of a new ethic which consists of caring for the patient as if he/she were a sick animal, not in accordance with its specific medical need, but according to the wishes of its master or owner—the person or entity responsible for paying the medical bills.[2]

For the first time in the history of medicine, physicians are being coaxed or coerced, whatever the individual case might be, to ration health care by restricting their patient's access to specialists or expensive treatments—that is, involuntary rationing for the sake of cost containment and as to make the HMOs, for which they work, more efficient and profitable.

Today, physicians are subject to so-called cost-effective analysis and *economic credentialing*. This is a methodology by which hospitals and health care networks (particularly HMOs) use utilization review data about physician medical practices (not to determine quality, but to monitor financial impact). Physicians who have not been cost-effective, that is, they have not been stringent in their restrictions (or who treat the sickest and most difficult cases and thereby incur the most costs in their communities), may have not only their bonuses withheld at the end of the year, but could also lose their membership status in hospitals or health care networks when they apply for new, additional, or renewal of clinical staff privileges.

Major health care networks are acting in collusion with government bureaucrats and policymakers to impose managed competition, and to change the time-honored ethics of the medical profession. Much about this cozy relationship between government bureaucrats and private health care megacorporations has come to light, at both the state and national levels.

At the state level, we have the case of Minnesota where a private foundation, working hand in hand with members of the governmental Interagency Working Groups, has instituted a bureaucratic, "Clinton-Lite," statewide health care system.[3]

At the national level, thanks to the lawsuit (*AAPS v. Clinton*) filed by the Association of American Physicians and Surgeons (AAPS) against the Health Care Task Force headed by Hillary Clinton and Ira Magaziner, we again have the case of corporate special interests seeking to change the American health care delivery system, to revamp it and make it more to their liking and directed towards their own financial benefit.[4,5] In both the state and national scenarios, big foundations and megacorporations, with a vested financial interest in managed care (HMOs), militated behind closed doors under the auspices of the government to implement managed competition as the method of health care delivery for the entire nation. The concept of managed competition (or *corporate socialized medicine*), with managed care and gatekeepers as centerpieces and cost containments as its *raison d'être*, threatens the supremacy and the sanctity of the patient-doctor relationship and the ability of the physician to do ethically all he/she can for his/her patients.

We must remain vigilant and cognizant that under the guise of cost containment, the health care debate during the rest of this decade does not deteriorate into incremental reforms directed at covert rationing of medical care, and that quality and technology are not sacrificed on the altar of expediency and deceit. With managed care, Dr. Thomas Dorman, an AAPS physician member from California, asserts that the profitable incentives for cost containment are so irresistible as to constitute "competition in rationing."[1] In fact, it can be argued that the whole scheme of managed competition is the profit motive for the megacorporations and competition in rationing for the rest of us.

The lessons of history sagaciously reveal wherever the government has sought to control medical care, medical practice, or physicians, the results have been as perverse as they have been disastrous. In our own century, in the Soviet Union and Nazi Germany, medicine regressed and descended to unprecedented barbarism in the hands of the state. Physicians must not falter at this crucial moment. We should not allow neither the government nor the powers that be (or corporate socialized medicine and managed competition) to change the noble ethics of the House of Medicine or adulterate the sanctity and trust of the patient-doctor relationship.

There is a threat of a modern dark age looming on the medical horizon. It is the impending dark age of corporate socialized medicine, and if this form of medical care is ever fully implemented in America, patients can rest assured they will be greatly affected. They will find that their new physicians dare not advise them what is best for them, but will do as they are told by government bureaucrats and/or government-controlled, token, third-party networks. Gone will be the independent-minded physicians of yore who took medicine to its pinnacle, free of government intrusion and coercion, who treated their patients as individuals and who placed their patients' interest above their own, in the spirit of true altruism, philanthropy, and humanitarianism, and within the sanctity of the patient-doctor relationship. Lost will be patient and physician autonomy.

The reality is that the government-inspired false "ethics of caring," is based on what is actually closer to Professor Truffer's veterinary ethics, an ethic that forces physicians to act in the interest of the government or corporate entity as third-party payer, rather than in the interest of their patients; mandates coercive compassion; responds only to pressure by politically-powerful special interests; and insists on statism and collectivism to solve the world's problems, rather than on the philosophical notion of free will and individual initiative.

For physicians, the impending change in the ethics of the medical profession, as it relates to the patient-doctor relationship, is of paramount importance. In fact, it is my profound belief that this transformation in the time-honored ethics of the patient-doctor relationship will be the defining issue for the rest of this decade. It will determine the physicians' place in the general scheme of things, both in the professional realm of medical practice, as well as in their civic and social position in society. Will they remain committed to their patients in the tradition of Hippocratic medicine (and for others to the Oath of Maimonides), or will they succumb to veterinary ethics and the specious notion of doing what is "best for society" (and the managed care entity that employs them)? Before answering this question, let us remember both Socrates' admonition, *nosce te ipsum*, "know thyself," as it pertains to our role as healers and physicians, and Hippocrates' counsel, *primum non nocere*, "first do no harm"—for the future of the profession and the health of our patients hang in the balance.

## REFERENCES

1. Dorman T. Managed care newsletter. San Luis Obispo, CA., February 1993.
2. Faria MA Jr. Vandals at the Gates of Medicine—Historic Perspectives on the Battle Over Health Care Reform. Hacienda Publishing, Inc., Macon, Georgia, 1995, pp. 240-242.
3. Hartsuch D. Beware of state health reform—inside Minnesota care. J Med Assoc Ga 1995;84(1):17-22.
4. Brown KM. Doctors fight government intervention with judicial activism. J Med Assoc Ga 1994;83(8):459-464.
5. Orient J. White House releases task force documents. J Med Assoc Ga 1994;83(12):711.

(APRIL, 1995)

## CHAPTER 23

# *THE MEDICAL GULAG*

*Acquiescence is the trademark of the slave.*
Aristotle (4th Century B.C.)

The issue of whether we will remain an independent and compassionate profession or become an enslaved government trade union will not be clearly evident until some time after the Presidential election. For one thing, the conservative health care planners have been silenced by the media, and the Congressional democrats (73%) favor socialized medicine either in the form of National Health Insurance (NHI) or Universal Medicare-type coverage (RBRVS) as previously advocated by Congressmen "Pete" Stark (D-CA) and Dan Rostenkowski (D-IL). So you ask, "What about the future of health care?"

We appear to be poised for a uniquely American version of socialized medicine—apparently, we do not learn from other people's mistakes. Moreover, to placate conservative critics, the health care reform package will have a veneer of "free-market" capitalism covering a hard core of socialism, RBRVS concepts and rationing.

From the capitalist school, we will be compassionately coerced to work twice as hard as before to make up for the decrease in reimbursement inherent to RBRVS. We will also be subjected to dogged competition and medicolegal litigation-on-demand. From the new school of Democratic Socialism, we will be imbued with the philosophy of equal suffering and the illusory dream (and entitlement mentality) of cradle-to-grave "free" care.

And here is the scenario: Assuming Clinton wins...either as a result of RBRVS implementation as the Democrats call it, or as a result of "managed care networks" with a "fixed amount of money for meeting the full needs of consumers," as Clinton calls it—health care costs will be brought down primarily at the expense of one group, the doctors.

Physicians, in fact, will be reimbursed 40% to 50% of their

present fee schedules, as well as continuing to be targeted for intimidation and scare tactics by enforcement of vague and cryptic rules and regulations—all as part of the *novus ordo seclorum* of health care delivery.

But what about decreased fees and productivity? It is well known that HCFA presupposes that less physician reimbursement (less compensation for their honest work) would result in "the [greedy] physicians" working twice, or maybe thrice, as hard to compensate for their lost income. Is this presupposition indeed correct? The answer is of paramount importance.

Let us look at a transcendental lesson from history. The great Russian patriot, Alexandr Solzhenitsyn, in his monumental work, *The Gulag Archipelago*, exposes an inescapable analogy that came to light in one of my many conversations with a dear friend who shares my inclinations in these philosophical and geopolitical matters. Solzhenitsyn wrote that there were two types of prisoners in the gulags: those who resisted and those who collaborated with the enemy by doing what they were told and working as hard as they were capable for the promised reward of extra rations. For their additional work, the collaborators were given a smidgen more of food, just enough to convince them they were better off than the others.

The bitter truth was the extra ration they received was not enough to provide the compensatory nourishment to sustain their intense labor. The irony of the situation was that the collaborators in the Soviet gulags unintentionally hastened their own demise by the accommodation of their tormentors and their acquiescence and complaisance in the face of their own predicament. They died off, never to see the Berlin Wall fall in November of 1989 or the Evil Empire disintegrate in January of 1991, as the whole world watched.

Likewise, in medicine, physicians beware. Let us not acquiesce, thereby hastening not only our personal demise, but also that of the noble profession of Medicine.

(DECEMBER, 1992)

## Chapter 24

# *Ethics, the AMA, and Lack of the "Vision Thing"*

*The physician should be contemptuous of money, interested in his work, self controlled, and just. Once he is in possession of these basic virtues, he will have all the others at his command as well.*[1]

Galen (2nd Century A.D.)

It has been repeatedly said both by physicians in the hospital lounges and medical commentators in the media that the AMA tries to please everyone and ends up pleasing no one. Is this commentary valid? And, if so, why?

In the opinion of this editor, for too long the AMA has tried to be all things to all people; and this attitude—namely, pragmatism at all cost—simple put, evinces a lack of vision, a lack of leadership, a lack of a moral compass, reflected in repeated flip-flops, not just in socioeconomic policies and health care affairs, but even more revealing, in ethical pronouncements.

### An Ethical Pronouncement

One morning as I was driving to Mercer University on my way to tutoring my first year medical school PBS (Problem Based Solving) group in the Neurology BMP (Neuroscience, Basic Medical Problems), I was first stupefied, then appalled, to hear the popular radio commentator, Paul Harvey say that a spokesman for the AMA had just issued a proclamation regarding "inappropriate touching" of female patients (presumably by male physicians) in the conduct of a physical examination in the doctor's office. According to Harvey, the AMA spokesman said that a woman "knows" when she has been touched inappropiately and should not be afraid to "step forward."[2] In other words, in the frenzied race towards political correctness, the AMA has once again shot off the foot of its membership, tossing away the presumption of innocence until proven guilty, for the sake of political expediency and projected public image.

And here, we should pause for a minute to realize that no

one is immune to this kind of accusation. The truth is that in this adversarial litigious society, it no longer makes a difference whether you are a man or a woman. In fact, in California, a multimillion dollar judgement was awarded to a Hispanic man who successfully claimed sexual harassment by his female boss.

Be that as it may, upon reaching my destination, I called the AMA to get their side of the story and for clarification of any possible misrepresentation. In short, I wanted to ascertain the veracity of the story. After listening carefully to what seemed to be an endless series of taped instructions and selections from the AMA phone "menu"(including a message in Spanish), my call was finally answered by a "live" voice. Before I could completely explain the reason for my call, I was transferred to membership. Knowing this was not the department I needed, I quickly explained the reason for my call. I was next transferred to a department I presume to be Public Relations or its equivalent. Finally, my call was transferred to Legal Affairs. I made my way to the secretary to the Chief Counsel and explained the business at hand. The secretary took down the information and said someone in legal counsel would call me back. No one ever did. (And, in a subsequent call, I was even told a member of the staff from the "women's organization" would call me, but again, no one ever did.)

### CIRCLING THE WAGONS

One could only arrive at the following explanation, one that historically has been played and replayed before—namely, that the AMA leadership was again circling its wagons and shooting inward against its own members.

In the meantime, we are not gaining any points in the political arena of health care affairs. With unspeakable horror, informed physicians are witnessing the step-by-step dismantling of our venerable profession with the malignant-like growth of managed care and veterinary ethics, the consolidation and vertical integration of health care delivery, erroneously attributed to free-market capitalism; more correctly, attributable to the growingly manifest iniquities of *corporate socialized medicine*. To add insult to injury, physicians in metropolitan areas are already trampling over each other to pay the $1000 enrollment fees charged by each and every managed care network (and HMO) that comes their way. They feel that if they don't, others will and wipe out their patient base. Yet, many complain bitterly about their rising professional dues. And, some even quit their professional organizations because of "bad economic times."

But what has led to this state of affairs? In many of my previous writings, I've alluded to the motley of different factors that have adversely impacted medical practice and our profession. Nevertheless, among these factors, one issue seems to recur time and again—*medical ethics*. All too often, instead of standing by our ideals, persevering in the pursuit of truth, following the time-honored principles set forth in the Oath of Hippocrates, and the ethical tradition of our medical forefathers, we have often been too willing and too eager to transmute the ethical precepts of our profession for the political expediency of the moment, and to apply quick pragmatic solutions in inept and short-sighted attempts at solving the political and ethical conundrums of our time.

As a result, organized medicine at the national level has lost significant influence, not to mention credibility in Washington for such activities as supporting political candidates on both sides of the fence and for frequently contributing to the campaign coffers of such foes of medicine as Rep. Fortney "Pete" Stark (D-CA).[3]

I've been told by at least one defender of this practice that this is "just politics!" That may be, but when we are dealing with principles rooted in ethics, the latter should not be compromised.

This may also explain why—despite the anxiety and uncertainty of the health system reform drive (1993-1994), driven as it was in the extreme leftward direction toward socialized medicine—the AMA was unable to seize the moment, provide a vision, and capitalize on the very issue to make significant gains in its membership at that very critical time.

## DRUG SAMPLES, SELF (AND FAMILY) TREATMENT AND PROFESSIONAL COURTESY

In 1994, the MAG House of Delegates (1994) passed over-whelmingly two resolutions dealing with specific medical ethics.

What is unique about these resolutions, submitted by two separate county medical societies, is that they contravened previous knee-jerk "ethical" pronouncements injudiciously passed by the AMA's Council on Ethical and Judicial Affairs. The resolutions, reproduced in their entirety, speak for themselves.

### Resolution 5
#### Ethical Stand on Free Drug Samples and Other Gifts (Trinkets) from Industry, Self and Family Treatment, and Professional Courtesy
#### (Bibb County Medical Society)

"WHEREAS, the media and sundry health care "pundits" have come out questioning or outright denouncing a variety of time-honored medical practices and ethics; and

"WHEREAS, the medical profession whose members (the vast majority) follow ethical principles 2500 years old and is the most policed and scrutinized profession in the U.S., yet, day in and day out, physicians' integrity is questioned (including the old and venerable practice of professional courtesy) by others who followed no such ethics, and physicians' autonomy is being usurped step-by-step; and

"WHEREAS, the leadership of our national organization, the AMA, has yielded much too often to the pressure of advocacy groups and tends to shoot inward towards the friendly wagons of its members, rather than outward, against our detractors [i.e., "AMA Opposes Free Drug Samples For Family Use"[4] and opposes physicians' treatment of family members.[5,6] Moreover, AMA guidelines for sponsorship of educational programs by pharmaceutical companies are unclear and subject to the political winds;[7-9] and

"WHEREAS, some insurers are already proclaiming that acceptance of payment from an insurance company but not the deductibles or copayments from a patient colleague should be not only unethical, but illegal;[10] and

"WHEREAS, AMA and MAG members may be affected adversely by such all-encompassing "ethical" pronouncements, including detrimental repercussions;[11] now, therefore be it

"RESOLVED, that MAG confirms that the voluntary

professional courtesy of treating colleagues and their families is part of the Hippocratic tradition, and therefore, an ethical practice which has bound practitioners since time immemorial, and which may contribute to the preservation of the integrity of the profession; and be it further

"RESOLVED, that free drug samples and other inexpensive gifts, given to physicians by pharmaceutical or other medical industries, or the sponsorship of events that promote medical education (and thereby, enhance medical practice and the well-being of our patients) by those entities, should not of themselves be considered unethical; and be it further

"RESOLVED, that the acceptance of pharmaceutical or small gift items from the pharmaceutical industry, or their use by physicians (and their families) not be considered by themselves "impermissible gifts," unless there is clear and convincing evidence to the contrary (i.e., pattern of substance abuse, etc.)—for there are not historical precedents to bolster such "ethical" pronouncements."

### RESOLUTION 11
### PERSONAL USE OF DRUG SAMPLES
### (DEKALB COUNTY MEDICAL SOCIETY)

"WHEREAS, the AMA recently informed physicians that it is not permissible for physicians to accept drug samples for personal use or use by a family member; and

"WHEREAS, the promulgation of such an absurd rule is an insult to the professional integrity of the medical profession; and

"WHEREAS, the opportunity to use newly approved medications or other drugs personally, for appropriate indications, can be beneficial to the physician indetermining his or her prescribing practices for patients; and

"WHEREAS, traditionally physicians have considered it perfectly ethical to evaluate and treat minor health problems for their families and themselves and have traditionally considered it perfectly ethical to use drug samples if indicated in the course of such treatment; now, therefore, be it

"RESOLVED, that MAG, through its delegation to the American Medical Association's House of Delegates, introduce a resolution which asks the AMA to request the Council on Ethical and Judicial Affairs of the AMA to reconsider its recent opinions on industry gift giving guidelines/opinions pertinent to:

"Guideline 1h—Gifts to Physicians From Industry: Drug samples for personal use or use by family members.

"Guideline 1i—Gifts to Physicians From Industry: The limits on allowed gifts at industry dinners.

"Opinion 8.19—Self-treatment or Treatment of Immediate Family Members."

Thanks to the foresight and the sensible and overwhelming vote of the House of Delegates the previous year (1993), our Constitution and Bylaws had been amended "so that the Board of Directors or House of Delegates could reject, modify, or change prevailing ethics or standards governing the conduct of members. Such rejections, modifications, or changes would then become the official position of the Association. As specific questions of principles and ethics develop, pronouncements from the Medical Association of Georgia [over the AMA] would be paramount."[12]

A word of caution: Although the term "prevailing ethics" may appear at *prima facie* to endorse situational ethics, it most certainly does not. Like the U. S. Constitution, the bylaws must be read and interpreted from both wording and original intent. The House of Delegates was not referring to amending absolute Hippocratic ethics or expressing conflict with the AMA Principles of Medical Ethics (1980) which are sound and true—but to expedient, newly genuflected "ethical" pronouncements and statements issued from time to time by the AMA that physicians in Georgia believe go against the grain of transcendental principles of medical ethics. This addition was necessary, because according to our bylaws, we are otherwise bound to the AMA Principles of Medical Ethics as well as any ethical pronouncement promulgated by the AMA, including those enunciated by the Council of Ethical and Judicial Affairs— future or present.

## THE MORAL OF THE STORY

Before we join the bandwagon of managed care and

borrow capital from the AMA to establish our own managed care physician-directed networks, let us remember at least one of the most outlandish flip-flops of only a few years ago,* when physicians had initially been given the blessing of the AMA, but then later, found themselves on shaky ethical and legal ground with the practice of joint ventures, including referrals to diagnostic entities in which they had a vested financial interest.[14]

So, given the AMA's past record on these tough, gray-zone areas of medical ethics, physicians should think twice before forming their own managed care networks. I caution you because if you do join these profit-seeking ventures, you will be traversing perilous waters, and, sooner than you think, you may find yourself in unsafe harbors and haunted by troubling questions of impropriety (and legalities). This is particularly true in Georgia, where, unlike insurers and non-physician run managed care entities, providers (including physicians) do not have any antitrust exemptions, and thus, are easy targets as "violators" of antitrust provisions.

Sadly, at this time, the AMA provides no valid cause for comfort, nor solid professional leadership based on principle rather than expediency, for navigating in the troubled waters in which we find ourselves. While correctly encouraging us (at the state level) to push for Patient Protection (formerly "Willing Provider") legislation, the AMA (at the national level) is encouraging physicians to join the rush of new ventures—this time, physician-run, managed care networks.[15]

But, I have a final *caveat emptor* for those of you who plan to jump aboard this latest maritime adventure; and that is, when the ship begins sinking and is quickly scuttled in ethical and legal rough seas, don't expect the AMA to be there to throw you a life preserver!

### REFERENCES

1.Faria MA Jr. Vandals at the Gates of Medicine—Historic Perspectives on the Battle Over Health Care Reform. Hacienda Publishing, Inc., Macon, Georgia, 1995, p.208.

2. Harvey P. Review of the News. WMAZ Radio, Macon, GA., May 10, 1995.

3. Faria MA Jr. On managed competition and other catch-22 items. J Med Assoc Ga

---

* Another flip-flop was the explicit contradiction between the obligation to treat or not to treat AIDS patients and its own AMA Code of Ethics, Principle VI, asserting the right of free association.[15]

1993;82(6):269-271.

4. Council on Ethical and Judicial Affairs. AMA. Gift to Physicians From Industry. JAMA 1991;265:501.

5. Hughes PH, Conard SE, et. al. Resident physician substance use in the United States. JAMA 1991;265(16):2069-2078.

6. Puma JL, Priest ER. Is there a doctor in the house. JAMA 1992;266(13):1810-1812.

7. Gorski TN. Doctors, drug companies, and gifts. Letter to the Editor. JAMA 1990; 263(16):2177.

8. Chren MM, Landefeld CS, Murray TH. Doctors, drug companies, and gifts. JAMA1989;262:3448-3451.

9. Glasson J. quoted by Page L. AMA opposes free drug samples for family use. Am Med News, January 24/31, 1994.

10. Tenery RM. Professional courtesy: An act of gratitude. Am Med News, March 8, 1993.

11. Berg RN. The ethical practice of medicine. J Med Assoc Ga 1990;79(11):863-864.

12. Bylaws of the Medical Association of Georgia. Chapter XIV, Section 1, Rules and Ethics.

13. Faria, op. cit., pp. 195-197.

14. Despite some overlap, ethical and legal issues of physician self-referral remain distinct. JAMA 1991;266(17):2335.

15. Peck P. AMA to help MDs find capital for networks. Internal Medicine News, March 15, 1995.

(APRIL, 1996)

## CHAPTER 25

# *TRUTH AND CONSEQUENCES*

*"It is not the critic who counts, not the man who points out how the strong man stumbled or where the doer of deeds could have done better. The credit belongs to the man who is actually in the arena, whose face is marred by the dust and sweat and blood; who strives valiantly; who errs and comes up short again and again, who knows the great enthusiasms, the great devotions and spends himself in a worthy cause; who at best knows in the end the triumph of high achievement; and who at the worst, if he fails, failed while daring greatly, so that his place will never be with those cold and timid souls, who know neither victory nor defeat."*
Theodore Roosevelt (1858-1919)

*Whosoever, aspiring, struggles on, for him there is salvation.*
Johann Wolfgang von Goethe (1749-1832)

### AT THE EXECUTIVE COMMITTEE MEETING...

I will never forget the events surrounding the dates of April 27-30, 1994. For in those days, I discussed the various issues surrounding my role as editor of the *Journal of the Medical Association of Georgia (J MAG)* and the direction, or rather, reaffirmation of the direction the *Journal* has taken in the last 14 months. I first discussed these issues with MAG's Executive Committee on Wednesday (April 27) and with the Board of Directors on the following day. To my satisfaction, the Executive Committee upheld the concept of journalistic independence and the need for the *Journal* to publish provocative medical articles (as long as they were of "quality" and supported by facts and logic) even if they went against the prevailing political winds.

We also reaffirmed: (1) That *J MAG* is a peer-reviewed journal. (2) That we welcome members who write articles and/or letters to the editor as to express the various points of views of the membership, including those who express contrary views to those presented in the *Journal*. Yet, we also discussed the fact that we must be cognizant to preserve and continuously upgrade the standards of a first-class publication such as the *Journal* and insist on quality regardless of the point of view. That by in large, we are a conservative organization and the *Journal*, overall, should reflect to some extent this fact.

And introspectively, of course, I thought about the reality of the hazards that accompany "the New Orthodoxy"—described by the scholar Thomas Sowell and "the New Intolerance" referred to by Supreme Court Justice Clarence Thomas[1]—that seeks to silence those in academia or in professional life who refuse to abide by the imposition of political correctness, and who persist in sailing against the prevailing political winds by overstepping the boundaries set by political expediency and political correctness.

In my view, an editor should strive not only to select material for publication as objectively as possible, in the quest for truth, and towards this end, seek out those points of view that have been suppressed or censored. An editor must also be open to counter points of view for the sake of fairness and intellectual honesty. For example, Dr. John E. Fowler, expressed the sentiment of many family practitioners and internists who support the concept of RBRVS. He believes this to be a necessary and fair tool to achieve pay equity within the medical profession. And thus, like Voltaire, although I disagreed with what he said, I defend vigorously his right to say it.* Thus, I spoke:

"The problem is that the most prestigious national medical journals including *JAMA* and *The New England Journal of Medicine* (*NEJM*), when dealing with socioeconomic and political issues have echoed the emotionalism and sensationalism of the popular press and electronic media—therefore often becoming a mouthpiece of the entrenched statist liberal establishment.

"A journal espousing a contrary view is needed to balance this torrent of conforming information and close this gap of knowledge. We hope the *Journal* can fill in this gap.

"Our journal is committed to publishing both scholarly review articles as well as op-ed commentaries to provide a forum for contrasting views, particularly contrary views, even if they go against the torrent of advocacy views, showered upon us, day in and

---

* In fact, later on, I edited for him a short commentary piece which was, "The only thing," he said, "I ever had published."

day out by the proponents of big government. There is in fact a window of opportunity for the *JMAG* to attain a place in the sun, precisely because *JAMA* and the *NEJM* have too often closed the curtain and kept us in the dark regarding conservative ideas and politically incorrect thought, and this includes health system reform. Compare all of the columns and pages alloted to the single-payer and managed care proposals versus medical savings account (MSA), the veritable last hope for the preservation and reinvigoration of private medical care via a truly free-market system. Yet, even when it comes to health care proposals, I recognize, as do most members of the Editorial Board, that when anyone takes a strong stand based on principles, it is impossible to satisfy and to have the support of the entire membership, particularly in such a group as independent-minded as physicians.

"The March issue of the *Journal* has been the most provocative and successful issue published to date, requiring a second printing to satisfy the needs and the thousands of requests from physicians and the public. If we want the *Journal* to succeed (and many state journals are not succeeding; the *New York State Journal*, for example, succumbed last year) and perhaps even be influential, *it must first be read.* And to be read it must be bold, provocative, and credible. Today the *Journal* is being read and read more than ever.

"We need to accomplish these necessary prerequisites by bringing to light views that have been suppressed or glossed over by other publications, as long as what we publish is factual information and is supported by objective data. For instance, the popular media and the medical literature have failed to report 'the other side' of the gun issue, the environment issue, or, as alluded to earlier, even the conservative proposals for health care reform. Little has been said about the explicit benefits of tax-free medical savings accounts (MSAs), and the fact that despite the tax allowance incurred by this proposal (as put forth by the Dallas-based National Center for Policy Analysis), the concept is estimated to result in savings of approximately $147 billion annually. Thus, expounding on this concept of MSAs coupled with high-deductible catastrophic insurance coverage, our June 1993 issue broke new ground with free-market medicine. At that time, that idea was a novelty in Georgia and most of the nation, even amongst physicians. Today, thanks to the *Journal*, many of us at MAG and in the public at large now believe it's an idea whose time has come.

"Then, in the August and September 1993 issues, we hit hard at the litigation juggernaut. Some of those ideas for curbing the liability crisis, including the *English Rule* ('loser pays all') and restricting attorney contingency fees with a sliding cap, have been incorporated in the major Republican health care proposals along with MSAs. Our sensational, influential, and highly requested December issue exposed the fallacy of the U.S. pursuing health care 'like in other countries.'[2]

"Our March through June 1994 issues admittedly contain contrary and thus, some would say, politically incorrect views. Nevertheless, these issues demonstrate that there is a legitimate viewpoint that is rarely given a forum in the medical journals, but which should be aired for public discussion. We welcome those with different points of view, recognizing that we do practice peer review but not censorship, as others (evidenced by their predictable, monotonous, and unswerving medical orthodoxy) obviously do in medical journalism, following the lead of *JAMA* and the *NEJM* when it comes to socioeconomic and political issues."

### At the Board of Directors Meeting...

On Thursday, April 28th, I gave my *Journal* report to the Board of Directors. In so many words, I expressed the fact that for too long physicians have been content with taking care of their patients in the trenches of health care delivery; this will no longer do. We have been working long and hard hours; and for this labor, we have been called "greedy" by government bureaucrats and politicians. I further went on to say:

"For remaining uninvolved and acquiescent, expecting others to do our bidding, look at what has happened to our profession. We are about to be swallowed by an increasingly omnipotent government authority with corporate socialized medicine and a myriad of regulatory and oppressive edicts—and our patients face involuntary medical care rationing. After 2500 years of independence, our profession is about to be enslaved by government bureaucrats using either the oxymoronic managed competition scheme of health care delivery or the false illusion of a single-payer system. If you don't believe me look at today's paper.[3] We can no longer afford to remain acquiescent and complaisant, while the best health care delivery system in the world is being dismantled, step-by-step.[4]

"The national medical journals—*JAMA* and the *NEJM*—time and again, cater to the emotionalism and sensationalism of the mass media, or echo the political expediency or political correctness of government bureaucrats. These journals, despite the expressed sentiments and wishes of the majority of physicians in the trenches who want to preserve the patient-doctor relationship, the practice of private medicine, and the independence of academic medicine have, in many instances, spearheaded efforts in health care reform in the wrong direction—that is, toward more government intrusion, and step-by-step, socialization....

"We want to reaffirm the benefits of private sector medicine, the benefits of the free exchange of information, the sanctity of the patient-doctor relationship—and take the lead in health system reform efforts, so that it proceeds in the right direction. To do this, we need to be widely read, and we must have the courage to tackle controversial issues objectively. Yet, we do not want to be divisive within the House of Medicine. Ultimately, we seek to increase the membership and to be unified under the banner of MAG.

"Moreover, as stated in the masthead, the views expressed by the editor and the specific authors represent their own individual views, and not necessarily the views of MAG. We must also keep in mind that, as history has taught us, the airing of contrary views is healthy and necessary in a free society. Censorship of opposing viewpoints often heralds the beginning of a not-so-free society and may signal an abject prelude to tyranny."*

## AT THE HOUSE OF DELEGATES...

Friday, April 29, and Saturday, April 30, were busy days at the House of Delegates assemblage. Delegates discussed and debated,

---

* Later, I was told by the Executive Director that I was the only speaker to receive an enthusiastic round of applause that long and drawn out Spring day of 1994.

pro and con, issues ranging from MSAs and the President's health care proposal to medical ethics (from professional courtesy, the acceptance of small gifts from pharmaceutical companies, to self and family treatment for minor and recurrent illness, etc.). Two resolutions that directly and indirectly involved the *Journal* sparked great debate.

One resolution dealt with the topic of guns and self-protection within the context of domestic and street violence. This resolution was "debated eloquently" by proponents as well as opponents of the measure in the Reference Committee. The resolution was endorsed by individual members from three separate county medical societies and the two most controversial Resolves finally approved by the House read as follows:

*[and be it further]*

*RESOLVED, that MAG uphold the credo that the Second Amendment protects the law-abiding citizen's right to "keep and bear arms" as to allow for personal and family protection [from the plight of single mothers who live alone with children and need protection at home to those involved in sports, e.g., marksmanship, hunting, and firearm collectors]; and be it further*

*RESOLVED, that MAG supports the important ideals of personal responsibility, moral guidance, and education, along with a tougher criminal justice system without revolving prison doors, especially for those committing crimes with firearms; and that MAG take the unequivocal position against the banning and confiscation of firearms from law-abiding citizens.*

Besides the fact that physicians, like everyone else, are concerned with issues of domestic violence and street crime, the resolution was also drafted because—as a result of the AMA and the mainstream medical journals, including *JAMA, NEJM,* taking public relation stands on a variety of issues including gun control—physicians in organized medicine at the state and local levels have also been called upon to advise and opine on these very same issues.

Be that as it may, to prevent further divisiveness within the House of Medicine (after all, our motto there was, "United We Stand, Divided We Fall"), a more moderate resolution was ultimately passed, and it was published in the July issue. It passed with some opposition from those in the House who either wanted to call for more stringent gun control measures, on the one hand, and those who wanted to return to a more strongly worded resolution, on the other.

The other resolution sought to remove the 3-year term limit that was instituted by an Ad Hoc Committee on Publications and approved by the Board of Directors before the present editor was appointed. A second Resolve to this resolution proposed that the editor "be commended for a job well done."

After some discussion, the resolution passed lifting the 3-year term limit, and the editor was "commended" for his service. I owe this commendation to those around me who supported me during the unexpected vicissitudes encountered during this momentous meeting. First, I thank my wife, Helen, for her encouragement (and for serving frequently as "my editor"); Ms. Susan Johnson, Managing Editor of the *Journal*, Dr. Bob Lanier, President of MAG, the Executive Committee, the Board of Directors, and Mr. Paul Shanor, Executive Director—for their unwavering support; the Editorial Board of the *Journal* for being a working board; the loyal readers of the *Journal* for their overwhelming positive response as exemplified by their deluge of phone calls and letters to the editor; and the MAG delegates on both sides of the debate—the supportive supermajority who have been delighted with the direction that the *Journal* has taken as well as those who have not—for the topic needed discussing and debating. I am also very grateful to all of those who extended their hand of friendship, particularly those who spoke on my behalf: Dr. Milton Johnson, Dr. Billie L. Jackson, and others who spoke in the Reference Committee that I may not be aware of. Thank you all for the overwhelming support, for I cherish the *Journal*, despite the many hours a week (of phone calls, correspondence, topic research, and writing, etc.) that it takes to put together a great journal such as ours.

It is obvious from the debate that all of us who are involved with the *Journal* still have a lot of work ahead of us. We have to do a better job presenting the other side of the story. The Editorial Board and I will only serve as long as we can be of benefit to MAG, our cherished *Journal*, and the House of Medicine—and for as long as the Board of Directors deem it so. In essence, we all have won, for as the Latin-American writer Juan Montalvo (1832-89), once wrote, "nothing is harder than the coldness of indifference." The reception the *Journal* has received in the last 18 months has been anything but indifferent, and according to our Managing Editor, unprecedented—and all who care about the *Journal* should be exalted that this is so.

## REFERENCES

1. Thomas C. The rule of law and the new intolerance. The Wall Street Journal, May 12, 1993. (Excerpted from his speeches given at Mercer University and the Georgia Public Policy Foundation in May 1993.)
2. Glasser WA. The United States needs a health system like other countries. JAMA 1993;270:980-984.
3. Single payer system picks up momentum. USA Today, April 28, 1994.
4. Faria MA Jr. Vandals at the Gates of Medicine—Historic Perspectives on the Battle over Health Care Reform. Hacienda Publishing, Inc., Macon, Georgia, 1995.

(AUGUST, 1994)

June 27, 1994

Miguel A. Faria, Jr., M.D., Editor
*Journal of the Medical Association of Georgia*
5791 Kentucky Downs Drive
Macon, GA 31210

Dear Dr. Faria,

On behalf of the Medical Association of Georgia, I thank you for your loyal work as the Editor of the *Journal of the Medical Association of Georgia.*

Your efforts to produce a *Journal* that includes provocative and high quality articles have certainly paid off. The *Journal* has become much better read -- due largely to your leadership as Editor. To your credit, recent articles have illuminated both sides of controversial issues and have initiated healthy debate among MAG members.

I commend you for the outstanding job you have done as the Editor of the *Journal* and appreciate the generous amount of time you spend providing this excellent service to organized medicine.

Sincerely,

Jeffrey Nugent, M.D.
Chairman, MAG Board of Directors

CHAPTER 26

# *REVIEW OF THE NEWS AND THE DIRECTION WE ARE HEADED*

*How many more patients will be lured into managed-care programs, only to discover that they are unwitting victims of health care rationing?*

*...How many more physicians will have to struggle to keep their practices financially afloat because of paltry HMO capitation fees? How many other physicians will have to struggle to avoid managed care related-malpractice suits?*

*In the interim, how many other physicians will leave the rank of the medical profession to become physician executives in the managed-care arena?*

Bernard Leo Remakus, M.D.
*Author, The Malpractice Epidemic*

## QUALITY OF CARE

What many of us feared about cost containment and rationing is coming to pass. The February 1995 issue of *The Georgia Healthcare News* reported on two recent studies—one at Harvard Medical School, the other by scientists at Duke University—that indicated that "health cost containment strategies restricting access to medical specialists can lead to lower quality of care for patients." In this instance, it was heart attack patients.

The first study suggests that heart attack patients do better when patients have access to effective drugs and appropriate cardiology consultations. The study by the Duke researchers found that Canadian patients do not do as well as their American counterparts after having a heart attack. Again, decrease access to heart specialists, and sparsity of high-technology procedures appear to be a major factor for the difference in outcomes.

## CORPORATE CONTROL OF MEDICINE

The aforementioned findings appear to be the same in psychiatry. A study of depressed patients, reported in the same issue, found that while restricting access to specialists (psychiatrists) reduces costs, it also "leads to poorer results for patients."

That same month in Minnesota, which remains a hotbed of managed care and HMO controversy, the largest HMO, Health Partner, "announced [it] would discourage doctors from prescribing Prozac—the best-selling antidepressant." The *Minneapolis Star Tribune* (Feb. 23, 1995) further reported that "doctors are expected to use two 'similar' and cheaper drugs." Therefore, it appears this action was taken, not because of quality concerns, but because of the corporate drive for cost-containment. Prozac has now been removed from the formulary of drugs that physicians in the network can prescribe for their patients.

Exceptions to this proscription will be made for those patients who are able to convince their gatekeepers they should be referred to psychiatrists, who, at least for the moment, will continue to be allowed to prescribe the drug.

The lesson that we are beginning to learn from these developments is that regardless of whether a corporate entity protected by government policies (i.e., managed care and HMOs), or the government itself (as the single-payer) is the culprit behind rationing—restricting choice of doctors, access to specialists and life-saving drugs or expensive technologies—the end result is the same: a rapid deterioration in the quality of care and the perversion of the Hippocratic ethic that requires physicians to place their patients' interest above cost consideration or any other consideration, including their own self-interest.[16] But the temptation to realize the bottom line in corporate socialized medicine,[7-8] appears to be too strong to be resisted. Despite rationing, cost-containment, the threat of lawsuits, and the perversion of the patient-doctor relationship, managed care and HMOs are thriving, increasing their market share and cash reserves by leaps and bounds.

*The Wall Street Journal* reported (May 18, 1994) that in 1993, U.S. Health showed a 16% profit, and Leonard Abramson, its CEO, received $9.8 million in salary, bonuses, and stock options. To add insult to inquiry, in *Business and Health* (November 1994), a survey of health insurance premiums paid by 1000 companies employing at least 200 workers—65% enrolled in HMOs—disclosed that the premiums had risen at double (4.6%) the overall inflation rate of 2.3%. No one, then, should be surprised by *The Wall Street Journal* follow-up report (Dec. 21, 1994) that in the past year alone (1994), liquid assets at many HMOs have climbed at 15% or more. "Thanks to rapid membership growth and slowing medical costs, many HMOs are pulling in money faster than they can spend it.'Our problem is what to do with the money that comes in, not whether we have enough cash,' says Alan Bond, director of treasury operations at Health Systems International Inc. in Pueblo, Colorado."

So it is not surprising that in our own state of Georgia, Blue Cross/Blue Shield (BC/BS) "goes for the gold," as Harriet Hiland reported in *The Georgia Healthcare News* (May 1995), meaning that the Georgia legislature has authorized by statute the formerly private, non-profit network to go public on its way to becoming a for-profit megacorporation and a full-fledged member of the "Big 5" health insurance companies, (replacing Metropolitan Life and Travelers which merged to form MetraHealth in February, 1995), and thereby, ending the only not-for-profit insurer in the state.

### AND, IT GETS WORSE...

Empire BC/BS, one of the largest Blues plans, announced last November that it would stop issuing new indemnity insurance policies "effective immediately" (*Business and Health*, January, 1995). What this means is that all enrollees will be herded into managed care plans that combine fee-for-service hospital services with an HMO option for all other health care needs.

The Blues' stampede toward managed care (HMOs) and for-profit status has paid off; and paid handsomely. *National Underwriter* (Oct. 17, 1994) asserted that "in October, the 69 BC/BS plans reported a combined enrollment in their HMOs (7.6 million people) that surpassed that of the seminal Kaiser Permanente HMO (6.62 million Americans). Presently, 42% of the Blues companies' total enrollment are in HMOs. This percentage continues to rise steadily."

Certainly, the direction that health care has taken has been in the direction of *managed competition*, the same direction that President Clinton had set in his Health Security Act of 1993, except that in this new corporate-government partnership (*corporate socialized medicine*), the power structure is leaning toward the side of corporate interests, while on the losing end, the collectivist-statist forces recover from the rout of the November '94 elections. Yes, the capitalist engine remains harnessed for rationing at the expense of the care ministered to sick patients and the labor of physicians in the trenches.[8]

As a result of this freight train headed full speed in the wrong direction, at least three major occurrences are (or are about) to take place. One, the Speaker of the U.S. House of Representatives, Newt Gingrich (R-GA), in a March 29th speech to the American Medical Association, called for a congressional investigation into managed care industry practices. The *AAPS News Legislative Bulletin* (May 1995) reported that the Speaker "thinks that managed care is accumulating vast financial powers and that corporate medicine is concerned more with the bottom line than with the quality of patient care."

Two, malpractice litigation has picked up steam. The largest windfall ever awarded in a Georgia medical liability lawsuit was delivered on February 2, 1995 by a Fulton County jury—$45 million against Kaiser Permanente of Georgia (*The Magnet*, MAG Mutual Insurance Company, March 5, 1995). "The case involved the HMO's decision to route a severely ill child to a hospital, 42 miles from his home." The medical center circumvented was known to be a premier children's hospital. During the car trip, the boy suffered cardiac arrest, lost circulation in his limbs, and eventually had to have his arms amputated. The jury agreed with the plaintiff's attorney that the child was sent to a distant hospital to save money and the HMO was to blame. The boy and his family were awarded $45 million.

Three, doctors are fleeing Minnesota—the mecca of managed care/managed competition, and the epicenter of corporate socialized medicine. At the last count, 2,300 physicians have fled the state since 1993 (*American Medical News*, April 10, 1995). Soon, unless we all say "no," there will be no sanctuaries remaining, for we will have reached the dead-end of managed care/managed competition. In all of America, then, physicians will be abjectly consigned to the medical gulag of corporate socialized medicine.

## WILL THE MEDICAL GULAG OF CORPORATE SOCIALIZED MEDICINE BE OUR FINAL DESTINATION?

"The issue of whether we will remain an independent and compassionate profession or become an enslaved government trade union will not be decided until some time after the Presidential election...We appear to be poised for a uniquely American version of socialized medicine—apparently, we do not learn from other people's mistakes. Moreover, to placate conservative critics, the health care reform package will have a veneer of capitalism [managed competition] covering a hard core of socialism [RBRVS concepts, rationing, capitation]...."[9]

### REFERENCES

1. Franzblau MJ. Ethical values in health care in 1995: lessons from the Nazi period. J Med Assoc Ga 1995;84(4):161-164.
2. Price TE. Why managed care won't last. J Med Assoc Ga 1995;84 (4):165-166.
3. Nirschl RP. Managed health care-patient protection or abuse? J Med Assoc Ga 1995;84(4):167-168.
4. Parish DC. Medical ethics and managed care. J Med Assoc Ga 1995;84(4):171-172.
5. Vincent RH. Pace of managed care leaves patients safeguards behind. J Med Assoc Ga 1995;84(4):175-178.
6. Domescik J. More on managed care. J Med Assoc Ga 1995;84(4): 182.
7. Faria MA Jr. Vandals at the Gates of Medicine—Historic Perspectives on the Battle Over Health Care Reform. Hacienda Publishing, Inc., Macon, Georgia, 1995.
8. Faria MA Jr. On the ethics of managed competition. J Med Assoc Ga 1995;84(4):159-160.
9. Faria MA Jr. The medical gulag. J Med Assoc Ga 1993;82(2):56. See Chapter 23.

(SEPTEMBER, 1995)

## CHAPTER 27

# CENSORSHIP AND EDITORIAL
# LYNCHING IN THE DEEP SOUTH

*Enemigos ¿No tienes enemigos? ¿Es que jamás dijiste la verdad, o jamás
amaste la justicia?*
(Enemies. You don't have enemies? Is it because you have never told the
truth or ever fought for justice?)

> Santiago Ramón y Cajal
> Spanish physician and Nobel Prize Winner in Medicine
> and Physiology, 1906 (for his work in neuropathology).

*[Note: On July 14, 1995, the Executive Committee of the Medical
Association of Georgia (represented by Drs. Alva Mayes and John Fowler)
asked for and received Dr. Faria's resignation as editor of the* Journal,
*because the editorial views expressed in the* Journal *had made "many
physicians uncomfortable and the leadership no longer wanted to take
the heat." Here is what transpired.]*

### SPEECH TO THE EXECUTIVE COMMITTEE OF THE
### MEDICAL ASSOCIATION OF GEORGIA

"Today, I will discuss the status of the *Journal of the
Medical Association of Georgia,* our premiere state medical journal.
I will discuss the budget and other items pertaining to the *Journal.*
Yet, before I do so, given the rumblings and the rumors, in the wake
of *The Atlanta Journal* editorial, I need to know if you are willing to
continue to strive to have the best state medical journal in the
nation, or whether you are going to abjectly capitulate and relinquish the position of leadership we have attained in the defense of
our patients and the quest for medical and scientific truth.

"Frankly, I suspect, not because of budgetary constraints,
but more likely, because of political intimidations from the infamous,
politicized, editorial in *The Atlanta Journal,* some of you may be
contemplating throwing in the towel. I hope, with all my heart, we
keep pressing forward for the preservation of what is left of the
sacred patient-doctor relationship, Hippocratic principles of
medical ethics, and journalistic freedom.

"We must not relinquish our responsibilities and our position of leadership in organized medicine and medical journalism. We owe it to our profession and to our patients not to give up at this difficult hour.

"We are truly at the crossroads of major health care changes, and you are going to need a strong journal with a strong and dedicated Editorial Board and editor who are willing to stand firm for journalistic excellence, and for truth and objectivity in medical reporting. And, we, the editor and the Editorial Board, are willing to do that and to take the heat for the organization.

"Today, health care megacorporations and managed care networks—including what even the AMA referred to as "the Gang of Five" insurers and Blue Cross/Blue Shield—would like nothing better than to break the resolve and unity of physicians and disperse their participation in patient advocacy. These megacorporations are making billions of dollars at the expense of physicians and the medical care of their patients—in fact so much capital and profits are rolling in their coffers, they admit they do not even know what to do with all the cash or how to spend it fast enough. Yet, they are silencing physicians with gag rules and denying patients access to quality medical care. That is why recently Kaiser Permanente lost $45 million in a lawsuit in Georgia and another $89 million in California. I suspect, though, given the health corporations' vast political and financial powers, it will be the doctors, particularly primary care physicians, who will eventually bear the brunt of the responsibility for the failures and ultimate collapse of managed health care. Physicians will pay dearly for the collapse of this false scaffold of medical care, with loss of credibility, and in the case of primary care physicians, with the lashing of the whip of the litigation juggernaut, as they assume wittingly or unwittingly, the dubious role of gatekeepers—but that is another story.

"Managed care entities do not want physicians involved in organized medicine, and already many physicians are not joining (or renewing their memberships in) their professional organizations because the HMOs and the managed care networks that employ them will not include their membership dues in their enrollment packages, or outright, discourage them from joining in organized medicine. Obviously, these HMOs want physicians disorganized so they can divide and conquer in Machiavellian fashion, as I have so frequently stated, as to force, eventually, all physicians to be salaried employees and then, in such an unnatural state, totally dependent on their government-approved employers.

"And again, it is being left to the *Journal of the Medical Association of Georgia* to bring to light this calamitous situation for physicians, while presenting all sides of the managed care debate—as we did in the April 1995 issue.

"Likewise, we have been the only journal to bring to light the activities of the powerful Robert Wood Johnson Foundation in Minnesota which, as you know, brought about corporate socialized medicine to that state working from behind the scene. We are on the cutting edge of medical journalism with the publication, time and again, issue after issue, of well-researched, scholarly articles on socio-economic and political issues affecting medicine. And while doing this, we have also stood tall for individual autonomy; the creation of a true free-market in medical care, in the form of medical savings accounts; free inquiry in the intellectual battle of ideas; the free flow and exchange of information; and the pursuit of medical and scientific truth.

"Since the last time I spoke to this body, I have spoken to many civic organizations, promoting our ideas and explaining our concerns. Yet, what I get asked, time and again, is why other doctors don't join the battle against managed care and against the loss of patient choice, which the public is now beginning to understand, not only as loss of *freedom* of choice, but also as medical rationing and deterioration of medical care. Our patients can not understand why physicians do not fight more enthusiastically for medical savings accounts, if this option, as we believe, may provide a viable solution. Interestingly, many have heard about our *Journal* and they are pleased to see we are taking stands on issues other than those that directly affect our pocketbooks. Believe me, when I tell you that when we do so, like the light of day, they know immediately we are standing for principles and not economic gain or political expediency.

"As far as the vicious editorial, you may want to ask yourselves, if we become intimidated by the first shot fired in our direction, particularly, by those who do not have the best interest of our profession at heart, and if we as physicians are going to be easily embarrassed in the heat of the debate because of our supposedly dignified position in society—then, we are poised to lose our independence, prone to capitulate our positions of leadership, surrender our ethics, and give up the time-honored privilege of being the true advocates for our patients.

"We must stand for the principles of our noble profession and our patients and our *Journal*, which as many members at the House of Delegates testified last April, was the 'heart and soul' of this organization.

"If we fail to stand by balanced and honest journalism, and our eternal quest for truth, we will be on our way toward professional extinction, unable to fight for our patients or our code of medical ethics. We will then become irrelevant, even if we manage to exist as a shell of an organization.

"The biased, inflammatory, and highly partisan editorial was intended to intimidate us. I hope instead it stiffens our resolve to fight for what we know is right. I, frankly, consider this unfounded attack a badge of honor for *The Atlanta Journal*, in my opinion, has never really been our friend or ally.* Rather, *The Atlanta Journal* has delighted in repeating the false mantra by calling us "greedy providers." They publish sensationalized stories involving alleged wrongdoings by physicians. And, they have opposed us on patient protection legislation which would have benefited patients, and of course, on antitrust relief (Amendment #3) which would have gone a long way to place physicians on a more level playing field when competing with insurance megacorporations, and thus, bringing down health care costs.

"What has the *Journal of the Medical Association of Georgia* accomplished?

(1) We are the premiere state medical journal. We have been cited in numerous periodicals and magazines outside of Georgia—this is almost unheard of for a state journal.

(2) We have presented a much-needed alternative to the

---

* On Sunday, June 18, 1995, *The Atlanta Journal* published a vituperative editorial entitled, "Journal With Disregard For Life," viciously attacking the *Journal of the Medical Association of Georgia* and me personally as the editor for daring to publish both sides of the gun control debate and expounding on it in the medical literature.

same rehashed, politicized medical views of other national medical journals.

(3) The *Journal* has been used in and distributed at informal seminars on managed care, as well as in more formal teaching courses (e.g., in International Health Care Strategies at Boston University).

(4) A member of the editorial board has now been asked to review grants intended for gun and violence research.

(5) The *Journal* is being read and praised by members of the Georgia Congressional delegation.

(6) We have praised public health for their work in combating truly epidemiologic diseases; yet, we have been critical when we feel they have deviated or failed to stand for truth, objectivity, and integrity in publicly-funded research.

Thank you."

(JULY 14, 1995)

After giving the aforementioned speech, several questions and comments ensued, but very quickly a motion was made for the Executive Committee to proceed into executive session and all non-members were excused. Before I left the meeting, Dr. Gwynn Brunt, Chairman of the Executive Committee, stated he was surprised how easy I went on my response to *The Atlanta Journal* (of course, he probably only read the two paragraphs the newspaper chose to print and not the full text of my letter). He also said he agreed "with most everything I said."

Dr. Ralph Tillman asked a very shallow and perfunctory question to the effect of why the *Journal* was not yet financially self-sufficient, and I explained we had made progress and gave figures to that effect.

Dr. Benjamin Cheek, a new member of the Executive Committee, presented a charade of a "survey" he took of his county medical society members regarding the *Journal* (of which, it seemed, less than a dozen responded): the largest group responding to his survey were for leaving the *Journal* as it was (in other words, they were happy with it), though that response was not even a choice in his "survey," and had to be written in. The choices were either for "changing the direction" or outright "killing" the *Journal*.

Dr. Roy Vandiver, a past president of MAG, defended the Journal and said that at the Dekalb Medical Society almost everyone had positive comments about the *Journal*.

Dr. Joe Bailey, another respected past president, also spoke about the need for unity and his concern for the dismemberment of the organization. He supported the *Journal* as did Dr. Vandiver (but they were no longer voting members of the Executive Committee).

Dr. Alva Mayes, the President, praised my speech and stated I had done a good job for the *Journal* ("the best editor the *Journal* ever had!").

Dr. Alan Plumber (who had written a letter to the president of reproach against me because of *The Atlanta Journal* editorial) remained mute.

My friend of many years, Dr. Tom Price, remained silent.

Mr. Paul Shanor, Executive Director of MAG, pointed out the fact that the *Journal* always attempted to present both sides of the issue. He also stated the angriest he had ever been was about a letter from a physician castigating the *Journal* for having "the audacity to discuss the other side of the gun debate." Mr. Shanor felt physicians were professionals, and if they could not stand to hear both sides of a scientific issue impacting on medicine, then they probably were in the wrong field!

Absent from this meeting was my friend and supporter, Dr. Bob Lanier, immediate past president of MAG.

Needless to say, after these remarks, I felt that of the three main issues to be addressed in the executive session, the lingering controversy of *The Atlanta Journal* editorial would be important, but perhaps not paramount.  I had, after all, weathered the storm the year before (after the March '94 issue) after the left-wing liberals had mounted a concerted all-out assault with letters (I published all of them) and speeches in the House of Delegates in an attempt, I was told, "to deliver my head on a platter."

The remaining two issues to be discussed concerning the *Journal* revolved around, (1) the appointment of a "controversial" (non-good-ol'-boy) member to the Editorial Board which was vehemently opposed by some high-ranking members within the organization, but whom I continued to support as I felt the opposition was unfair and uncalled for; and (2) concerns about further budget cuts affecting the *Journal* as MAG was expected to lose 500 members due to the managed care economic impact on physicians.

Later that evening, my wife and I conversed at dinner with our friends, Drs. Bill and Billie L. Jackson. In the course of the pleasant conversation, I jokingly stated that since the Executive Committee had gone into executive session, there was a chance we would lose our jobs. (Dr. Billie Jackson was a member of the *Journal's* Editorial Board.) However, on balance, I felt I had presented a plain and fair overview of what the *Journal* had done and tried to accomplish, and most members of the Executive Committee gave the impression or, at least appeared, if not actually stated, to have acceded to my report. In any case, I was in for a big, unpleasant, late evening surprise.

At exactly 11:05 p.m., while in the midst of reading *Cuban Childhood Memoirs* by Pablo Medina, we, my wife, Helen, and our little daughter, Elenita, who was already asleep in bed, and I, were startled by a phone call. On the other end of the telephone line was Dr. Alva Mayes, MAG President, who tersely asked me to come to Room #124 to speak with him and Dr. John Fowler, MAG Chairman of the Board of Trustees.

When I arrived, with tension building in the air, they politely told me that unanimously or almost unanimously (they disagreed on that account; 7 members with 1 possibly abstaining), the Executive Committee (and in violation of the Bylaws of MAG*) had voted to ask for my resignation. In doing so, Dr. Mayes said he felt in "an awkward situation" not only because he was "my friend" and had recommended my appointment as editor, but even more importantly and significantly, because he felt I had done an "outstanding job with the *Journal!*"

So why, and to what gods, had I been sacrificed, then? The answer: "I was making too many physicians uncomfortable."

To that reply, amidst the fog of deception and disbelief, I remembered thinking to myself:

*Eureka, the public and media were right on this one. Physicians, despite the devotion of some, and long hours of*

---

* Under the MAG Bylaws, the appointment and term of office of the Editor and the Editorial Board is under the jurisdiction of the MAG Board of Directors, not the Executive Committee.

*others, want to ply their trade making a good living, but 'they don't want to make waves,' or in any way, stir the powers-that-be, bringing attention to themselves. It's no wonder, then, through the ages, Francois Rabelais, Jonathan Swift, and particularly, Moliere had such a great following, satirizing human, and particularly, as with Moliere, physician folly!*

So, in my unpleasant reverie, I further pondered:

*We must no longer care about right or wrong. We have reached the point, where the physicians of organized medicine, from the AMA trickling down to my own state medical association, had taken upon themselves the heavy burden of capitulation. Yes, in so many word, I was being told that the leadership didn't want to deal with social and political issues that made them uncomfortable [or threatened their still comfortable economic position and aloof, dignified status in their communities].*

As Dr. Fowler admitted, "We [the leadership], frankly, just don't want to take the heat!"

The "leadership," particularly with many of them now becoming officers in health networks and investing financially in managed care, and the Editorial Board and myself declaring managed care the #1 problem facing the medical profession, it became apparent the *Journal* with this editor posed a threat to the leadership, a leadership who yearned not to fight for their patients, but rather, to preserve their financial security and their filigrees of power concomitant to their political offices in organized medicine, adjusting to change by applying situational (not medical) ethics, as they go, and using pragmatism as their guiding moral light.

And so, first the *Journal* with budget cuts and then its editor (my Editorial Board would later be quietly dismissed) with a late night, sudden usurpation, suddenly and without warning, had both been swiftly sacrificed on the altar of political expediency!

The rest is history, and the occasion of my editorial lynching in the Deep South proved again George Orwell's maxim: "In this age, there is no such thing as 'staying out of politics,' all issues are political issues."

(July 16, 1995)

BUILDING A BETTER STATE OF HEALTH

Office of the President

October 6, 1995

Miguel Faria, M.D.
5791 Kentucky Downs Drive
Macon, Georgia  31210

Dear Miguel:

I write at the request of the MAG Board of Directors to commend you for your service as Editor of the <u>Journal of the Medical Association of Georgia</u> during the past three years.

I, personally, and the Board feel that the <u>Journal</u> grew progressively during your tenure as Editor, and we are grateful for your service.

I regret very much that we were not able to continue our relationship.

Best wishes to you and your family in the future.

With best regards,

                                        Sincerely,

                                        A.L.

                                        A. L. Mayes, Jr., M.D.
                                        President

ALM/dg

938 Peachtree Street, NE  ■  Atlanta, GA 30309-3990  ■  404.876.7535  ■  1.800.282.0224  ■  fax 404.874.8651

# SELECTED BIBLIOGRAPHY

1. Annis ER. Code Blue—Health Care in Crisis. Regnery Gateway, Washington, DC, 1993.
2. Bastiat F. The Law (1850). Reprinted by The Foundation for Economic Education, Inc. (1990), Irvington-on-Hudson, New York, 10533.
3. Brown KM. Doctors fight government intervention with judicial activism. J Med Assoc Ga 1994;83(8):459-464.
4. Farber S. The real abuse. National Review 1993;45(7):44-50.
5. Faria MA Jr. Crisis in health care delivery—rescuing medicine from the clutches of government. J Med Assoc Ga 1992;81(11):615-620.
6. Faria MA Jr. The litigation juggernaut. Part I: The dimensions of the devastation. J Med Assoc Ga 1993;82(8):393-398, and Part II: Strategies and tactics for victory. J Med Assoc Ga 1993;82(9):447-451.
7. Faria MA Jr. Vandals at the Gates of Medicine—Historic Perspective on the Battle Over Health Care Reform. Hacienda Publishing, Inc., Macon, Georgia, 1995.
8. Fumento M. The Myth of Heterosexual AIDS. New York, Basic Books Publishers, 1990.
9. Goodman JC and Musgrave GL. Patient Power—The Free Enterprise Alternative to Clinton's Health Plan. CATO Institute, Washington, DC, 1994.
10. Goodman WE. Health care in Canada: face-to-face with reality. J Med Assoc Ga 1993;82(12):647-649.
11. Griffin GE. The Creature from Jekyll Island. American Opinion Publishing, Inc.,
12. Grigg WN. The politics of child abuse. The New American 1992;8(18):23-30.
13. Hartsuch D. Beware of state health reform—inside Minnesota care. J Med Assoc Ga 1995;84(1):17-22.
14. Hiatt N and Hiatt JR. A history of life expectancy in two developed countries. The Pharos 1992;Spring:2-60.
15. Hunt JG (ed.). The Essential Thomas Jefferson. Gramercy Books, New York, Avenel, 1994.
16. Journal of the Medical Association of Georgia—Special Issue. Health Systems Abroad: Are They Right for America? December 1993.

17. Journal of the Medical Association of Georgia—Special Issue. Guns a Failure of Peer Review. March 1994.

18. Journal of the Medical Association of Georgia—Special Issue. Managed Care Symposeum. April 1995.

19. Kates DB and Harris PT. How to make their day. National Review 1991;43(19):30-32.

20. Kleck G. Point Blank—Guns and Violence in America. New York, Aldine de Gruyter, 1991.

21. Krug EC. Save the planet, sacrifice the people—the environmental party's bid for power. Imprimis 1991;20(7):1-5.

22. Lee RW. Free Medicine. The New American 1991. The New American, P.O. Box 8040, Appleton, WI. 54913.

23. Lowry R. Samuelson R. How many battered children? National Review 1993;45(7):46.

24. McCaughey E. No exit: are you really ready for the Clinton Health Care Plan? The New Republic 1994;February 7:21-25.

25. McManus JF. Financial Terrorism—Highjacking America Under the Treat of Bankruptcy. Western Island, Appleton, WI, 1993.

26. The New American—Special Issue. Regulation in America—Is this Still the Land of the Free? May 1993. American Opinion Book Services, P.O. Box 8040, Appleton, WI. 54913.

27. The New American—Special Issue. The Resilient Earth. June 1992. American Opinion Book Services, P.O. Box 8040, Appleton, WI. 54913.

28. The New American—Special Issue. The Clinton Cure-All—A Trauma to American Health Care. November 1993. American Opinion Book Services, P.O. Box 8040, Appleton, WI. 54913.

29. Norbeck TB. Telling the truth about rising health care costs. Private Practice 1990;22(2).

30. Olson WK. The Litigation Explosion—What Happened When American Unleashed the Lawsuit. Truman Talley Books, Dutton, New York, 1991.

31. Orient JM. White House releases task force documents. J Med Assoc Ga 1994;83(12):711.

32. Orient JM. Your Doctor Is Not In—Healthy Skepticism about National Health Care. Crown Publishing, Inc., New York, 1994. Available from the author. 1-800-635-1196. AAPS, 1601 N. Tucson Blvd, Suite 9, Tucson, AZ. 85716.

33. Panati C. Extraordinary Endings of Practically Everything and Everybody. New York, Harper and Row Publishers, New York, 1989.

34. Percival T. Medical Ethics. Chauncey D. Leake (ed.), Williams and Wilkins Co., Baltimore, MD, 1927.

35. Rand A. Atlas Shrugged. Signet Books, 1957.

36. Ray DL and Guzzo L. Trashing the Planet. Harper Pernnial, 1992.

37. Solzhenitzyn AI. The Gulag Archipelago. Harper and Row Publishers, New York, 1973.

38. Suter EA. Guns in the medical literature—a failure of peer review. J Med Assoc Ga 1994;83(13):133-148.

39. Suter EA, Waters WC IV, Murray GB, et al. Violence in America—effective solutions. J Med Assoc Ga 1995;84(6):253-263.

40. Wolinsky H and Brune T. The Serpent on the Staff—The Unhealthy Politics of the American Medical Association. G.P. Putnam's Sons, New York, 1994.

# *INDEX*